Laurence Olivier
on Screen

Laurence Olivier

Laurence Olivier on Screen

FOSTER HIRSCH

A DA CAPO PAPERBACK

Library of Congress Cataloging in Publication Data

Hirsch, Foster.
  Laurence Olivier on screen.

  (A Da Capo paperback)
  Reprint. Originally published; Laurence Olivier.
Boston: Twayne Publishers, 1979. (Twayne's theatrical
arts series) With new foreword.
  Bibliography: p.
  Filmography: p.
  Includes index.
  1. Olivier, Laurence, 1907–   . I. Title.
PN2598.O55H5   1984   791.43′028′0924 [B]   83-25516
ISBN 0-306-80211-2 (pbk.)

This Da Capo Press paperback edition of *Laurence Oliver on Screen*
is a republication, with updated entries and a new foreword, of the book
entitled *Laurence Olivier* published in Boston in 1979. It is reprinted by
arrangement with G. K. Hall & Co.

Published by Da Capo Press, Inc.
A Subsidiary of Plenum Publishing Corporation
233 Spring Street, New York, N.Y. 10013

Contents

By Foster Hirsch

A Method to Their Madness: The History of the Actors Studio
The Dark Side of the Screen: Film Noir
Love, Sex, Death, and the Meaning of Life:
Woody Allen's Comedy
Joseph Losey
The Hollywood Epic
A Portrait of the Artist: The Plays of Tennessee Williams
Who's Afraid of Edward Albee?
George Kelly
Edward G. Robinson
Elizabeth Taylor
Beyond the Horizon: American Theatre in the Twenties
(in preparation)

Foreword to the Da Capo Edition

"LAURENCE OLIVIER is incredibly bad as General MacArthur," a friend of mine called to tell me, fresh from a press screening of *Inchon*. "His performance is so hammy and so misconceived that the audience kept laughing at him. Really, it makes you want to look at his work all over again, to see if he was as good as everyone always said he was."

Knowing my admiration for Olivier, my friend was being deliberately provocative, issuing a challenge he didn't really mean. But his report did send me at once to see a film I had had no intention of seeing, since my objections to its producer, the convicted felon Reverend Moon, had overridden my regard for Olivier. My friend was right on one count, though quite mistaken on another: Olivier's MacArthur was indeed a failure, a bad performance of a kind that I think only a great actor can manage; but seeing it only underscored the indestructibility of the actor's lifetime accomplishment. A silly performance in a loathesome film (and what *was* Olivier doing working for Reverend Moon? How can he possibly account for it, even on the grounds of financial need?) cannot dislodge him from his place in the history of the art of acting. In *Inchon*, *Dracula, The Jazz Singer, Clash of the Titans,* and *A Little Romance*, his movie performances since the first edition of this book was published in 1979, the century's foremost actor seems determined to test our loyalty; but a string of campy character parts in mass market pulp cannot erode or qualify the beauty of his Henry V and Richard III and Othello, his Archie Rice and Macheath and James Tyrone.

Olivier belongs to history, but he refuses to ossify. He's an ambitious, working actor who will not be buried alive behind his awesome reputation. And so, despite battles with three life-threatening diseases, and in the face of sometimes extreme physical pain, Olivier has continued to act because, obviously, that is what he loves to do. Each time we see him, he looks increasingly frail, so physically diminished and vulnerable that he seems like a token of human mortality; and yet there he is, acting with vigor if not always with taste, and insisting on doing all his stunts, even when they would be risky for an actor in his prime. Because much of his recent work is not top quality (though most of his co-workers and critics are too dazzled by the tyranny of his reputation to say so), Olivier's eagerness to add credits to his canon is a little discouraging; but there is another way to look at his ongoing productivity, and that's as a sign of heroic resilience, the power of a terrific stubborn will.

When an artist past his peak goes on being creative, his work can usually take one of two directions: it can become drastically simplified, as if he is giving us the essence of what he knows, or it can become increasingly mannerist, as the artist relies on tricks he has acquired over the course of a lifetime. Olivier in his senior years tends to fall into the latter category, as he regales us with technique, besieging his roles, no matter how threadbare or conventional, no matter how minor the character or the film, with an avalanche of detail. Now more than ever, Olivier exults in showing off his skill. He wants us to catch him acting.

Consider two recent accent parts of the kind he relishes: the debonair French pickpocket in *A Little Romance,* and the orthodox rabbi in *The Jazz Singer.* In *A Little Romance* his role immediately calls up memories of Maurice Chevalier; he is all dewy Gallic charm. Playing a coy, superannuated boulevardier who spins tall tales of a romantic past to two impressionable youngsters, Olivier wrinkles his nose, rolls his eyes, pours on a thick accent, garnishes his dialogue with sweeping hand movements. It all looks like an acting exercise, Olivier savoring the tools of his craft. In *The Jazz Singer,* he's also out of his element. If you're Jewish, you can feel in your bones that Olivier isn't, and that his idea of a rabbi is a goyish one. In a part that George Jessel or Eddie Cantor could have bathed in Jewish ethos, Olivier is artificial: his attempt at the Jewish schmaltz the sappy story calls for simply isn't the real thing.

Olivier's only substantial work in recent years has been on television, as the aged Lord Marchmain in *Brideshead Revisited;* as a tyrannical blind judge in *Voyage Round My Father;* and in *King Lear.* All three are full-bodied, genuine performances, a world apart from the actorish stunts of the recent movies. As the dying Lord Marchmain, steeped in memories, Olivier is wonderfully intimate, lining his character's words with nuance and shadow. In contrast, his gruff domestic tyrant in *Voyage Round My Father* has the sudden volcanic eruptions and the piercing irony that have been part of most of his major performances.

Olivier's Lear is not definitive, and it certainly shouldn't be judged as a valedictory or as the distillation of a lifetime dedicated to scaling the Shakespearean summits, but the performance is nonetheless stamped with the actor's characteristic fearlessness. He makes Lear starkly unheroic, a man on the edge of an abyss. Foolish, doddering, dim-witted, slow of gait and speech, distracted, this Lear seems exactly the kind of old man who would do something so ill-considered as to give away his kingdom. Except for occasional flashes of cunning, there is almost no reminiscence in this frail, senile figure of the monarch Lear must once have been.

We can't but notice Olivier's diminished vocal and physical resources, and his work is sabotaged by indifferent direction and a set design lacking in atmosphere or thematic reinforcement, but Olivier's acting is lit by the keen psychological insight that all his truest performances have had. Seeing his Lear is to be reminded once again that Olivier's power is not finally based on disguise or externals but on his skill as a student of human behavior. He may begin with a mental picture of what his character looks like, and how he moves and sounds, but these are only ways for allowing him to enter into the character's mind. The physical details stimulate Olivier's investigations of his character's inner life, and in all of his most far-reaching work he ends up in the same place as the inner-directed Method actor whose technique he has always quite vocally opposed: revealing a character's spirit. Olivier's accents, wigs, facial hair, false noses, limps are really the equivalent of the Method actor's use of private moments, and emotional and sensory recall, ways to prod his imagination about what's going on inside his character, beneath the surface level of words and actions. The best Olivier, like the best Marlon Brando or Kim Stanley or Al Pacino or Geraldine Page, illuminates a character's complexity and ambivalence.

The conflict between living up to the demands of being the great Olivier on the one hand and the desire to assert his merely human fallibility on the other is the true subject of his 1982 autobiography, *Confessions of an Actor*. As much as anything, Olivier seems to have written the book (which is clearly in his own voice: no ghostwriters for him) to disprove the popular notion that a great actor has the obligation to be a great man. Sometimes, when he gives the public what it expects, he's surpassingly modest, formal, politic, playing superbly a gracious, well-spoken Lord Olivier. When he drops the public mask, however, he can be bracingly acerbic, as in his recollections of Lee and Paula Strasberg and Marilyn Monroe, and in his forthright account of his torturous relationship with Vivien Leigh, in which he seems equal parts ardent lover, cad, and martyr.

Far sturdier than most celebrity books, *Confessions* still isn't quite good enough. Olivier is too often detained by incidental anecdotes and personal gripes; and on acting technique, and perceptions about his own work, he is curiously reserved and fragmentary. (Though I suppose if he could have written about creating Othello as powerfully as he performed him, he would have been a writer rather than an actor.)

Reading the memoir, then, is to be presented with differing versions of Laurence Olivier—the regal actor and the flawed private man don't always seem to be closely connected, and finally, after the occasionally candid revelations, the insinuating self-deflations that are really a form of self-praise, the sporadic humor and charm, the man behind the illustrious career is as blurred, as shrouded from public scrutiny, as he's always been. The considerable sleight-of-hand achievement of Olivier's autobiography is that after seeming to tell all, Olivier as himself remains in opaque soft focus, the expert actor manipulating his role and his audience.

—FOSTER HIRSCH

New York, October 1983

Preface

"WHAT IS THE MAIN PROBLEM OF THE ACTOR?" Laurence Olivier was asked in a recent interview. "It is to keep the audience awake," he answered promptly. "Keep them surprised; shout when they're not expecting it; keep them on their toes—change from minute to minute."[1] Wooing the audience with the unexpected for over fifty years, Olivier has built his career on being audacious and original. The actor has always been enchanted by risks, and his work is studded with vaudevillian turns, elaborate displays of technique, virtuoso transformations of voice and appearance and manner. A master of disguise, Olivier has performed with a variety of noses, wigs, beards, mustaches, eyebrows, and lips. Camouflaging his natural good looks, he has been fat and old, scraggly and gap-toothed, decadent, sinister, reptilian. To fit the demands of a role, he has grown tall and he has shrunk, and he has raised and lowered his natural voice by at least an octave. Compulsively applying makeup and adapting himself to a wide range of characters, he has successfully hidden the "real" Laurence Olivier from view: how is it possible to separate the man from the actor's many masks?

"Acting is illusion, as much illusion as magic is, and not so much a matter of *being* real," Olivier has said.[2] Unlike Method actors, whom he describes as being "entirely preoccupied with feeling real to themselves instead of creating the illusion of reality," Olivier constructs his characters from the outside in, beginning with a strong visual concept, with one or two external details—a limp, a shuffle, a slump; a flowing wig, a prominent nose; a stutter, a drawl. Rather than depending on instinct or self-investigation, Olivier relies on external technique.

In a recent book of interviews with people who have worked with Olivier, Alan Webb recalls a moment from *Titus Andronicus* that pinpoints the actor's method. After having worked up the audience to a fevered state, Olivier is about to chop off his hand with an axe, and as he prepares for the self-mutilation, he turns upstage. What is going through his mind during this moment of theatrical frenzy? How does he prepare himself for the bloody act that is to come? How deeply has he allowed himself to get into his part? Though Olivier has transported the audience and his fellow actors, he has not as it turns out relinquished control over his own emotions, for at the height of his torrential outpouring he whispers urgently to the actor who is sharing the stage with him, "Get out of my light! "[3]

The incident vividly demonstrates the technical control that underlies Olivier's power. The actor is a master of artifice who fools us into believing that he is "lost" in his role. Olivier is a brilliant faker, a cunning trickster whose startling transformations are the result of an almost scientific detachment.

Olivier challenged the genteel tradition in classical acting; from his earliest performances critics placed him in the realistic school of Edmund Kean as opposed to the remote and academic style of John Philip Kemble. By refusing to declaim or to recite Shakespeare's poetry and by introducing naturalistic rhythms, sudden leaps and drops in pitch and volume, and a variety of harsh sounds including shrieks and squeals, he played against the melody of the verse. Though he is certainly capable of beautiful readings, experimentation with meter and unlyrical outbursts have remained a part of Olivier's approach to classical roles.

Since 1935, when he and John Gielgud alternated the roles of Romeo and Mercutio in Gielgud's production of *Romeo and Juliet,* critics have often cast Olivier as the romantic Kean to Gielgud's classical Kemble, as "the burgundy to Gielgud's claret," the thunder and lightning to Gielgud's lyric recitalist. "I've always thought that John and I were the reverses of the same coin," Olivier has said. "I've seen the top half as John, all spirituality, all beauty, all abstract things, and myself all earth, blood, humanity—if you like, the baser part of humanity."[4] In contrast to Gielgud, who is rarely impressive visually, and who moves stiffly, Olivier has always been an intensely physical actor. Ethereal and introspective, Gielgud played the definitive Hamlet of his generation, while Olivier has never been entirely successful with brooding, withdrawn characters.

The comparisons with Gielgud remind us that, for all Olivier's versatility, he is not infinitely flexible. For all his range and resourcefulness, he is still best suited to particular kinds of roles. The great Olivier performances are as commanding figures of authority, courageous leaders of men, forceful orators, kings, soldiers, statesmen. Swaggerers, warmongers, extroverted public figures like Coriolanus, Hotspur, Henry V, Richard III, Othello—these release the actor's full power. Characters like Richard III who are themselves skillful actors; rulers whose lives are always on public display like Henry V; would-be tyrants driven by ambition like Macbeth—these larger-than-life characters allow for the rages and eruptions, the grandiose gestures, the dynamic energy, that are the hallmarks of the classical Olivier performance. As Kenneth Tynan has noted, "The characters that Olivier plays that most express his deepest self are people who want to rule and dominate and are prevented eventually from doing so. . . . He has this bottled violence which is what gives him this great authority onstage—gives his acting a sense of danger."[5]

Acknowledgments

PATRICK SHEEHAN and Joe Balian at the Library of Congress; William K. Everson; Ted Sennett; Michael Stephens at Channel 5, New York; Charles Silver at The Museum of Modern Art Film Study Center; the staff of the Theater Collection at the Lincoln Center Library of the Performing Arts, New York; the staff of the Academy of Motion Picture Arts and Sciences Library, Beverly Hills; Ann Hirsch and Renee Czeladnicki for compiling the filmography; Bill O'Connell, Ltd., for the photographs.

Chronology

England and *Twenty-One Days Together*, films with Vivien Leigh.

1938   Second Old Vic season (title role in *Macbeth*, Iago in *Othello*, title role in *Coriolanus*); *The Divorce of Lady X* (film).

1939   Healthcliff in film of *Wuthering Heights*; on stage as Gaylord Easterbrook in *No Time for Comedy*, with Katharine Cornell in New York.

1940   Directs himself and Vivien Leigh in *Romeo and Juliet* on the New York stage; stars on film as Darcy in *Pride and Prejudice* and as Maxim de Winter in *Rebecca*; marries Vivien Leigh, in California.

1941   Lord Nelson in *That Hamilton Woman* (film); *The Invaders* (film).

1944   Appointed Codirector of the Old Vic with Ralph Richardson and John Burrell; appears as Sergius in *Arms and the Man;* the Button Moulder in *Peer Gynt*, title role in *Richard III*.

1945   Directs *Henry V* on film. Second Old Vic season: Astrov in *Uncle Vanya*, Hotspur, Justice Shallow, in *Henry IV, Parts One and Two*, title role in *Oedipus* and Mr. Puff in *The Critic*.

1946   With the Old Vic in New York, in *Uncle Vanya*, *Oedipus*, *The Critic*, *Henry IV, Parts One and Two;* title role in *King Lear* with the Old Vic in London.

1947   Receives knighthood for services to stage and films.

1948   Directs *Hamlet* on film.

1949   With the Old Vic in London, in *Richard III* and as Sir Peter Teazle in *The School for Scandal;* directs Vivien Leigh in *A Streetcar Named Desire* in London.

1950   Actor-Manager at the St. James Theatre, London.

1951   Caesar in *Caesar and Cleopatra* and Antony in *Antony and Cleopatra* in London and New York.

1953   MacHeath in *The Beggar's Opera* (film).

1955   Directs *Richard III* on film; Malvolio in *Twelfth Night*, title role in *Macbeth* and in *Titus Andronicus* at the Shakespeare Memorial Theatre, Stratford-on-Avon.

1957   Archie Rice in John Osborne's *The Entertainer* at the Royal Court Theatre; directs and stars with Marilyn Monroe in *The Prince and the Showgirl* (film).

1959   At Stratford-on-Avon in *Coriolanus;* General Johnny Burgoyne in George Bernard Shaw's *The Devil's Disciple* (film).

1960   Berenger in Ionesco's *Rhinoceros* at the Royal Court; Crassus in *Spartacus* (film); Archie Rice in *The Entertainer* (film); title role in *Becket* on New York stage.

1961   Divorces Vivien Leigh, marries Joan Plowright; appointed director of Chichester Festival Theatre; Astrov in *Uncle Vanya* at Chichester; stars in *Semi-Detached* in London.

1962   *Term of Trial* (film).

1963   Appointed Director of the National Theatre; appears there as Astrov and as Captain Brazen in *The Recruiting Officer;* directs Peter O'Toole in *Hamlet.*

1964   Title role in *Othello* at the National.

1965   Bunny Lake Is Missing (film); Tattle in *Love for Love* at the National Theatre.

1966   *Othello* (film); *Khartoum* (film).

1967   Edgar in Strindberg's *The Dance of Death* at the National; directs Chekhov's *Three Sisters.*

1968   Films *The Dance of Death; The Shoes of the Fisherman* (films).

1969   *The Battle of Britain* and *Oh! What a Lovely War* (films).

1970   Created Baron Olivier in the Birthday Honors List; directs film version of *Three Sisters;* Shylock in *The Merchant of Venice* at the National; Creakle in *David Copperfield* (TV-film).

1971   James Tyrone in *Long Day's Journey into Night* at the National; *Nicholas and Alexandra* (film).

1972   *Sleuth* (film).

1973   *Lady Caroline Lamb* (film).

1975   *Love Among the Ruins* (TV-film with Katharine Hepburn).

1976   *Marathon Man*, Dr. Moriarty in *The Seven Per Cent Solution* (films).

1977   *A Bridge Too Far* (film).

1978   *The Betsy, The Boys from Brazil* (films).

1979   *A Little Romance, Dracula* (films).

1980   *Inchon* (film released in 1982), *The Jazz Singer* (film).

1981   *Brideshead Revisited* (television), *Clash of the Titans* (film).

1982   *Voyage Round My Father* (television), *Confesisons of an Actor* (autobiography)

1983   *King Lear* (television), *The Ebony Tower* (film, in production).

1

A Life in the Theater

WHEN THE LEGENDARY nineteenth-century actress Ellen Terry saw the ten-year-old Olivier in a school production of *Julius Caesar*, she wrote in her diary that "the small boy who played Brutus is already a great actor."[1] This story of early achievement, which has become part of the Olivier myth, conforms to all of the biographical information about Olivier which emphasizes that he was always motivated to attain distinction as a performer and that he has never wanted any public identity apart from that of "actor." The private man has indeed always remained concealed beneath the public image of Olivier, actor of stature. He has been among the least self-revealing of celebrated theatrical personalities; and so our sense of what he is like offstage is shadowy and incomplete.

To the question, "What is Olivier really like?" there have been wildly contradictory answers. He has been accused of excessive arrogance and extreme humility. He has been described as aloof and gregarious, intelligent and dim, self-serving and philanthropic, petty and vindictive on the one hand and extraordinarily generous on the other. Some fellow performers have said he is remote and others have said that he is reluctant to pull rank, preferring to be part of the ensemble rather than to strut before his colleagues as the lordly majordomo. The temperamental and emotional qualities that have been attributed to him over the years form a composite picture of a typical actor, compulsively wearing a mask both offstage and on. He has played his part so well that even his associates have never been able to tell exactly who he is. In the public consciousness he has never been thought of as anything but a distinguished man of the theater.

When, after his first great film success in *Wuthering Heights*,

The Oliviers: Laurence Olivier and Vivien Leigh as Admiral Lord Nelson and Lady Hamilton in That Hamilton Woman *(1941).*

19

Olivier was appearing in New York in 1939 in *No Time for Comedy* with Katharine Cornell, reporters, struggling to find story angles for this most elusive of celebrities, wrote that the actor disdained giving interviews because he was afraid of being misquoted. Olivier's distrust of the press at this time was triggered by an embarrassing incident: a gossip columnist quoted him as being bored with the play and with his costar. As John Cottrell notes in his biography of Olivier, "It was tame, inconsequential stuff . . . trivial pop journalism that no intelligent reader could take seriously. But it touched a sensitive nerve and Olivier overreacted, withdrawing tortoise-like into his austere English shell and refusing to come out . . . . The experience left a permanent scar on him, and his deep-rooted distrust of the press can be traced back to this point."[2]

Olivier has continued to keep a low public profile, seldom granting interviews and then only to appear before the press in a "role"—as director of the National Theatre, for instance, or as Eminent Actor. With no such part to play, with no clearly defined role as theatrical manager or institutional representative to shield him, he has jealously guarded his privacy.

Olivier has been married three times: to Jill Esmond (in 1930), to Vivien Leigh (in 1940), and to Joan Plowright (in 1961). Significantly, his wives have all been serious actresses, committed to the classics rather than to films or to popular modern drama. In public, his marriages have been conducted with suitable decorum. His romance with Vivien Leigh was celestial: the Oliviers, as they were called, led a glamorous life, with their medieval country estate, their elegant town house, their glittering social engagements. Throughout this most public phase of his life, however, Olivier avoided publicity as often as possible, remaining a dignified, remote figure, his first commitment always to his art. Both the beginning and the end of his relationship with Vivien Leigh were tinged with scandal (they were both already married to others when they first began seeing each other), and yet Olivier remained above reproach, untainted by the concentrated glare of public curiosity, dedicating himself to his work with heroic single-mindedness.

Olivier has cultivated his image as a consummate actor devoted with a kind of monastic zeal to the development of his interpretive skills. His arduous preparations for a new role became newsworthy items, taking precedence over glimpses into his private life. Olivier's method of transforming himself into his idea of Othello in

1964, for instance, was treated as an event of great cultural significance: man and career were linked inextricably in the public mind.

Early Years

What we know about Olivier's life, then, is closely connected to what we know about his development as an actor. Olivier always wanted to be an actor, and he was fortunate in having encouragement from his father, a clergyman of severe disposition who was apparently something of a ham himself. In a great deep voice of which he was immensely proud, the Reverend Gerard Kerr Olivier delivered his sermons with unmistakably theatrical flair. He was a remote father and the young Olivier looked to his mother for emotional support. When she died suddenly, Laurence, who was only thirteen, felt a keen sense of abandonment. He has said, in one of the few self-revealing personal statements he has ever made, that he has been looking for his mother ever since.[3] Certainly his warm memories of her have contributed to his good feelings for women and his need always to be involved in a romantic relationship.

Father and son had so little communication that Olivier was surprised when, in 1924, after his older brother left for India and he was alone with his father, the latter announced that, of course, Laurence was going to have a career on the stage. The secretive clergyman had never publicly acknowledged his son's achievements at All Saints School (where, in addition to Brutus, Olivier had played Katharine in *The Taming of the Shrew* and Maria in *Twelfth Night*), but he approved of his son's interest in theater.

With parental sanction, then, Olivier entered the Central School of Speech and Drama, under the direction of the formidable Elsie Fogarty, a homely, eccentric woman who inspired her students. Miss Fogarty's specialty was elocution, and her prize students (who included Peggy Ashcroft and Ralph Richardson, in addition to Olivier) testify to the rigor and the excellence of the training she offered. At his audition for admission to the school, Miss Fogarty gently reprimanded Olivier for his excessive gestures and told him, running a finger from his forehead to the bridge of his nose, that he had a "weakness" there. Both comments had the power of prophecy, for Olivier has proven indeed to be a highly physical actor—the use of his body has always been an essential part of his characterizations—and he has repeatedly disguised the "weakness" that Miss Fogarty noticed by wearing a remarkable assortment of false noses and wigs that changed the shape of his face. Olivier has always delighted in makeup as a kind of reconstructive surgery that transformed his natural appearance.

After his period of training at the Central School, Olivier divided his time between performing in classical drama in provincial repertory and appearances in ephemeral plays for commercial West End managements. In this respect this early phase set the typical pattern of his entire career. Devoted primarily to the classics and to the concept of repertory, with its emphasis on ensemble acting rather than star turns, Olivier was also mindful of the glamour and privilege of being a star. As a precaution against going stale in his classical roles, he has, throughout his career, tested himself in contemporary plays (and in films) of varying merit and seriousness.

In the 1920s, in the West End, he showed little judgment in his choice of plays. Since his main objective, as a novice actor, was to be employed, to be visible, he took whatever was offered. Most of these plays had only brief runs, and Olivier achieved no particular distinction in any of them. The greatest boost to his career came not from his superficial work in popular drama, but from his association with Barry Jackson's Birmingham Repertory Company. Jackson, like Elsie Fogarty (and, later in Olivier's career, Lillian Bayliss, director of the Old Vic), was a lover of theater whose fierce dedication provided both model and inspiration for the direction of Olivier's own work. Jackson never abandoned his visionary scheme of provincial repertory, even in the face of often-crippling economics. His Birmingham Company, which maintained notably high standards, provided a valuable apprenticeship in the classics for many performers later to distinguish themselves in London. Jackson had a practiced eye for spotting theatrical promise—he was impressed by Olivier, despite the fact that the fledgling actor, at the time, had done nothing of note.

In London, in 1926, Olivier played in Barry Jackson's version of a French mystery play, *The Marvellous History of St. Bernard*; in 1927, in Birmingham, he appeared as Tony Lumpkin in *She Stoops to Conquer* and as Monsieur Parolles in *All's Well that Ends Well*; and in 1928, at the Royal Court Theatre in London, he played the Young Man in Elmer Rice's expressionist drama *The Adding Machine*, Malcolm in a modern-dress version of *Macbeth*, the Lord in *The Taming of the Shrew*, and the title role in Tennyson's rarely performed closet drama *Harold.* The 1928 appearances with the Birmingham Company at the Royal Court afforded Olivier his first major exposure. He was particularly praised for his scrupulous Bowery accent in *The Adding Machine.* In a typically audacious maneuver, he had approached Claire Eames, an American actress appearing in London in *The Silver Cord,* to ask her to coach him on his "Americanese." She did, and as a result, Olivier was singled out in a small role for his dialectal authenticity.

Olivier's performances during this time were brash and exuberant. In a headlong effort to attract attention to himself, he had a tendency to overstate, to show off. His colleague Cedric Hardwicke later recalled that he was "noisy and lacking in subtlety. . .but I knew instinctively that he'd be a great actor."[4]

In this early period, Olivier was attracted to glamour and celebrity in a way he has never been since. Despite his work with Jackson's company, he was primarily interested at the time in a commercial West End career. One of his earliest successes was in 1928 as the romantic lead in an engaging, lightweight comedy by John Drinkwater called *Bird in Hand.* The handsome young actor played the lord of the manor who falls in love with a woman beneath his class. In this comedy of misalliance, written in a diluted Shavian manner, Olivier simply had to be charming, to smile, to move gracefully, to suggest a pleasing manliness. His goal in 1929 was to win the leading role in a spectacular romantic melodrama called *Beau Geste.* He felt that the part of the swashbuckling hero would establish him as a star: the young Olivier wanted to be a matinee idol. In order to get the role, he grew what was known at the time as a Ronald Colman mustache, and he cultivated the stance of a dashing, dark-haired romantic hero. Over many competitors, Olivier won the role, but the play was not a hit; if it had been, the actor might well have become a star, and his subsequent career as a preeminent classical actor might have been thwarted.

Because he had the qualities necessary for stardom—good looks and a potent sexual appeal—Olivier had similar brushes with fame throughout a good part of his career. In the case of *Beau Geste,* he was "saved" from stardom by the play's failure; later, after his enormous success in motion pictures as Heathcliff in *Wuthering Heights* (1939), Olivier himself rejected the temptations of Hollywood celebrity by acting at the Old Vic. Since *Beau Geste,* however, Olivier has occasionally returned to popular entertainments as

part of a deliberate policy of renewal and revitalization, as a preven-
tion against turning into a moldy, cloistered classical actor out of
touch with current trends.

Olivier's career in the late 1920s began shakily in a number of
formula plays (thrillers, melodramas, romantic comedies) that had
only short runs. He did not appear in a successful production until
Noel Coward signed him for the thankless second-man role in *Private Lives* (1930). Olivier, reluctantly, played the country bumpkin
to Coward's witty, debonair hero. Olivier agreed to accept the role
only after Coward warned him that he had better be in a hit. Appearing with Coward and Gertrude Lawrence in the brittle high
comedy proved valuable to the young actor; by close study, he
absorbed some of Coward's sophisticated manner, his deft comic
timing, his beguiling insouciance. Under Coward's masterful guid-
ance, Olivier began to lose some of the rough edges, the amateurish
exaggeration, that had marked most of his work up to this point.

After he "graduated" from the school of Coward, Olivier went on
to score a genuine success of his own in popular theater when he
played the character modeled on John Barrymore in *The Royal
Family*, by George Kaufman and Edna Ferber, a satire of the "royal
family of Broadway," the Barrymores. Maurice Barrymore and his
three famous children, John, Ethel, and Lionel, were the most
colorful theatrical family in American theater history. Tempestuous,
high-strung, their lives and careers marked by triumph and tragedy,
the Barrymores conformed to popular notions about the excesses
and debaucheries of theater people: Maurice died in an asylum,
suffering from an advanced case of syphilis; John became a hopeless
alcoholic whose career descended from the heights of an acclaimed
Hamlet to grotesque self-parodies in worthless exploitation dramas.
Playing the character modeled on a dashing young John Barrymore,
Olivier set out to dazzle audiences with his exuberantly physical
acting; Felix Barker recalls that Olivier "twirled his mustache at the
ends, made an entrance with two Borzoi, fought a duel on the stage,
leapt over a balcony, and gave a gutsy, eye-blazing performance
which invariably brought down the house."[5] To flaunt his versatility, he followed his athletic performance in the Kaufman-Ferber
comedy (called *Theatre Royal* in England, so audiences wouldn't
think the play was about the British royal family) with a potboiler
called *The Ringmaster*, in which he played an embittered cripple in
a wheel chair.

Later in the 1930s, seasoned by his apprenticeship with Coward, Olivier was notably pleasing in drawing-room comedy. His easy manner and his light voice qualified him for the *bon ton* of Philip Barry's *Paris Bound* and S. N. Behrman's *Biography*. In 1939, in his first starring role on Broadway, he appeared in Behrman's *No Time for Comedy* as a playwright who concocts glittering, frivolous entertainments for the carriage trade. Behrman's high comedy is a defense of urbanity and worldliness, and its theme summarized one aspect of Olivier's early career.

It wasn't until 1935, when John Gielgud asked him to alternate Romeo and Mercutio, that Olivier attempted a major role in Shakespeare; and it wasn't until nearly ten years later, when he managed the Old Vic along with Ralph Richardson and John Burrell after the war, that his reputation as a classical actor was assured. In the first twenty years of his career, then, Olivier spent more time in commercial plays than in Shakespeare. He was the English counterpart to the Boulevard actor or the Broadway star.

Though in London Olivier mixed popular plays with Shakespeare, on Broadway he wasn't recognized as a classical actor until the Old Vic season in 1946. Before that, his roles in New York, with one exception, had been in purely commercial vehicles: a thriller, *Murder on the Second Floor* (1929); *Private Lives* (1931); *The Green Bay Tree* (1934), in which he was a glamorous houseboy for a decadent art patron; and *No Time for Comedy*. When he appeared with Vivien Leigh in *Romeo and Juliet* in 1940, most of the critics felt that Heathcliff and Scarlett O'Hara had ventured beyond their depth; both actors were haughtily dismissed as movie stars who could not handle Shakespeare's poetry. John Mason Brown, who was to hail Olivier six years later, wrote that he "darts about boldly and manfully and he is always a romantic and picturesque figure, but his performance is singularly lacking in emotion and eloquence. . . . His Romeo is part Fairbanks–Robin Hood, part Jitterbug, part Frankenstein."[6]

Olivier's work in popular theater in the 1920s and early 1930s was self-consciously flamboyant. He built his reputation by being daring and outrageous, by flaunting his technical ingenuity and his gymnastic skills. His performances were usually marked by an elaborate accent or kind of movement or use of makeup and costume that forced the audience to take notice of him. In his work in the classics during this early period, he employed the same kind of emphatic and convention-smashing approach. He insisted on challenging popular preconceptions about the way classic parts should be played.

In his first major Shakespearean performance, as Romeo, he startled conservative West End audiences by playing Shakespeare's romantic hero as a hot-blooded youth. With sultry looks and lovesick sighs, he treated the language as contemporary dialogue rather than poetry. In a frequently quoted witticism, James Agate chided, "Mr. Olivier does not speak poetry badly, he does not speak it at all."[7] "His blank verse is the blankest I ever heard," sniffed the critic for the *Evening Standard*. The *Sunday Times* suggested that "Mr. Olivier's Romeo suffered enormously from the fact that the spoken poetry of the part eluded him. In his delivery he brought off a twofold inexpertness which approached virtuosity—that of gabbling all the words in a line and uttering each line as a staccato whole cut off from its fellows."[8] While most of the critics complained that his rough, erratic handling of meter stifled Shakespeare's music, a few were openly impressed by his daring departure from tradition. Tyrone Guthrie thought his Romeo had "speed and intelligence and muscularity," and he invited Olivier to join the Old Vic of which he was then the managing director.

"Not yet quite thirty," Guthrie recalled in his autobiography, *A Life in the Theatre*, "[Olivier] had already had considerable success both in New York and London and was on the threshold of fame. Offstage he was not notably handsome or striking, but with make-up he could achieve a flashing Italianate, rather saturnine, but fascinating appearance. The voice already had a marvelous ringing baritone brilliance at the top; he spoke with a beautiful and aristocratic accent, with keen intelligence and a strong sense of rhythm. He moved with catlike agility. He had, if anything, too strong an instinct for the sort of theatrical effect which is striking and memorable. From the first moment of the first rehearsal [of *Hamlet*] it was evident that here was no ordinary actor, not everyone's cup of tea—no very strong personality can be that; not necessarily well cast for Hamlet, but inevitably destined for the very top of the tree."[9]

Olivier remained at the Old Vic for two seasons, from January 1937 to April 1938. Under Guthrie's direction in the first season, he appeared as Hamlet, as Sir Toby Belch in *Twelfth Night*, and as Henry V. For the second season, he played Macbeth (opposite Judith Anderson, directed by Michael Saint-Denis), Iago (directed by Guthrie), and Coriolanus (directed by Lewis Casson, with Sybil Thorndike as Volumnia). Olivier's achievement in this first sustained experience in Shakespearean interpretation was considerable. Only his vigorous Henry V and his equally stentorian Coriolanus were unqualified successes, but all of his performances had vitality; all were startling in their aggressive originality, their attempts to be striking and radical.

Olivier was ideally suited to the outsized heroics of Henry and Coriolanus, two of Shakespeare's noblest warriors. Guthrie was especially proud of his spectacular production of *Henry V:* "It was the spring of 1937 and the Coronation of King George VI was imminent. We thought that a ringingly patriotic Henry V would be appropriate and that Olivier would be well suited to the part. It was, and he was."[10] Olivier, however, preferred Coriolanus to Henry because the role of the Roman soldier had the dark shadings and psychological complexity missing in Shakespeare's mostly idealized portrait of Henry. Coriolanus is exactly the kind of warped hero that Olivier has always found attractive, whereas he was bored with Henry's comparative balance and self-control.

His Sir Toby was played in a broad comic style, providing a thorough contrast both visually and aurally to his imperial Henry. Guthrie dismisses this *Twelfth Night* as "a baddish, immature production of mine, with Olivier outrageously amusing. . .and a very young Alec Guinness less outrageous and more amusing as Sir Andrew."[11] Disguised beyond recognition, and padded to Falstaffian proportions, Olivier as a rollicking low-comedy Toby Belch unbalanced the play.

His Oedipal Hamlet and his homosexual Iago were similarly unorthodox. Guthrie and Olivier were both intrigued by Ernest Jones's Freudian readings of the two plays, and they decided to incorporate elements of Jones's radical sexual interpretations into their productions. Olivier played Hamlet, as he had played Romeo, as a young man of ardor and instinctive, smoldering passions. James Agate quipped that his sexy, athletic Hamlet was the best performance of Hotspur he had ever seen. With Guthrie's collusion, Olivier stressed the sexual tension in Hamlet's scenes with a nubile, seductive Gertrude. (In June 1937, with Vivien Leigh as Ophelia, Olivier and Guthrie took their unconventional *Hamlet* to Elsinore, Denmark, playing it in the courtyard at Kronborg Castle, where it was enthusiastically received.)

Olivier's Iago was less persuasive partly because he and Guthrie were afraid to tell Ralph Richardson, their Othello, of their theory about Iago's sexual attraction to and sexual jealousy of the Moor. They felt Richardson would scoff at their notion. They introduced the homosexual overtones reticently, therefore, and with an uncooperative and unknowing Othello, their interpretation was doomed.

Patently designed to titillate, these early performances—excepting the martial Henry and the extroverted, tormented Coriolanus, which was capped by an astounding leap from a raised platform onto the stage floor—were not fully mature. Olivier was still a comparative newcomer to Shakespeare, and his work tended to be too striking and picturesque, marred by a natural exuberance not yet sufficiently under control.

Sir Laurence Olivier

After the war, in his second (and now legendary) association with the Old Vic, Olivier's technique was equally dazzling, equally virtuoso, but it had deepened and matured, almost as if his brushes with film-acting had corrected his tendency to overstatement, had chastened and subdued his bravura showmanship, adding a pleasing mellowness to offset the vaudevillian flourishes that were virtually by now an Olivier trademark. In this most spectacular phase of his career, from 1944 to 1946, he played an astonishing variety of roles. He was a melancholy, world-weary, yet charming Astrov in *Uncle Vanya*. In *Henry IV, Part I*, he played a virile, passionate Hotspur, who stammered on the letter "w," and in *Henry IV, Part II*, he depicted a wizened, spinsterish Justice Shallow. From one night to the next, Olivier's physique seemed to undergo a magical transformation. As Hotspur, he seemed larger than himself; as Shallow, he appeared withered and diminished. In his second *coup de théâtre*, he dramatically altered his image on the same bill. A fifteen-minute intermission separated his awesome Oedipus from his mincing Mr. Puff in Sheridan's *The Critic*. Performing the two roles back to back was a brash demonstration of virtuosity, and some critics accused Olivier of being vulgar. To these fastidious commentators, Sheridan's brittle comedy seemed an impertinence after Olivier's majestic reading of Sophocles's tragedy. But most critics and audiences were stunned. The piercing cries that accompanied Oedipus's terrible self-recognition are perhaps Olivier's most famous acting moment. His shrieks sounded like a slain animal's final agony, and theatergoers felt they were seeing the enactment of an elemental grief. The moment epitomized an Olivier trademark of reaching for peaks of high emotion in which his explosions of rage or despair challenge the limits of the character, the play, and the audience.

In a review that has become almost as well-remembered as Olivier's performance, John Mason Brown certified the actor's claim to greatness:

No word spills more infrequently or reluctantly than it does from any critical pen. For everyone's sake, for the well-being of the art involved, in the interests of criticism, out of respect for the language, and in defense of standards, "great" is an adjective which ought to be kept buried in the deep freeze. . . . But Mr. Olivier's Oedipus, considered along with his Henry V and judged in the light of his earlier contributions to the Old Vic, has left me no other choice. . . . I can only say that in *Henry V* and *Oedipus* I have seen the sun rise. And I refuse to mistake it for the moon, or salute it as such, when for me it is the sun. Mr. Olivier's Oedipus is one of those performances in which blood and electricity are somehow mixed. It pulls lightning down from the sky. It is as awesome, dwarfing, and appalling as one of nature's angriest displays. Though thrilling, it never loses its majesty. His Theban king is godlike in appearance. . .sullen, willful, august, and imperious. There is something of the young Napoleon in him too, but he is a Napoleon pursued by the Furies rather than following the Eagle.

About Oedipus's cries of self-recognition, when the character can no longer deny the fact that he is the killer of his father and that he has married his mother and had two children by her, Brown writes: "When the fearful realization at last inundates him . . . Mr. Olivier releases two cries which no one who has heard them can hope to forget. They are the dreadful, hoarse groans of a wounded animal. They well up out of a body that has been clubbed by fate. They are sounds which speak, as no words could, for a soul torn by horror, for a mind numbed by what it has been forced to comprehend. . . . The subsequent moments when Oedipus appears, self-blinded with the blood trickling down his face, are almost more terrible than audiences can bear."[12]

Equal to his achievement as Oedipus was Olivier's Richard III, a characterization which released the actor's mordant humor, his flair for garish melodrama, and his ability to evoke pathos from the unlikeliest characters. With his lank, stringy black hair, his sallow complexion, his beaky nose, his hunchback, his limp, and his reedy voice, Richard III is perhaps the actor's most dazzling mask. The character's evident delight in his deceptions, in his skill as a performer, matched Olivier's own joy in manipulating his audience. Olivier has said that his performance as Richard was the first time that he felt complete control over an audience, the first time that he felt in possession of an almost hypnotic power.

These Old Vic seasons established Olivier's reputation. In 1947, while filming *Hamlet*, he was knighted for his achievements in the theater. Although he has not since had a period of comparable incandescence, Olivier has, of course, continued to be a dynamic and often startling classical actor. For each of his major roles, he discovered a provocative concept that revealed new qualities about the character he was playing. He was too young for Lear when he played the part in 1946, but he introduced a dry comic tone in the early passages that many critics recall with appreciation. His driven, exhausted Macbeth, his craggy Titus Andronicus (at Stratford in 1955), and his petulant Coriolanus (at Stratford in 1959) are generally considered the finest modern interpretations of these roles. At the National Theatre in 1964, Olivier risked outraging audiences and critics by playing Othello as a black man, complete with rolling gait, crinkly hair, basso profundo voice, and thickened lips. And at the National in 1970, he stripped Shylock of the sentimentality that has become customary for the role by enacting him instead as a man possessed by spite.

Olivier, however, did not want to be typed as a temperamental classical actor, and in the late 1940s, after his triumphant seasons with the Old Vic, when his position as a Shakespearean performer was secure, he went into management at the St. James Theatre, where he presented a series of ambitious but mostly unsuccessful modern plays (beginning with Christopher Fry's opaque *Venus Observed*). In the late 1950s, Olivier went to the Royal Court to appear in John Osborne's *The Entertainer*. He wanted to be a part of the modernist atmosphere that dominated the Court Theatre in order to correct his image as a remote classical actor, and he claimed that his work at the Court "altered entirely the color and tone of my career at a time when it was becoming dangerously a little bit more staid and a little bit more predictable."[13]

Olivier's management of the National Theatre at the Old Vic (from 1963 to 1973) was marked by its hospitality to iconoclastic contemporary plays as well as modern interpretations of classics. Olivier wanted to keep up with the latest developments in theatrical style, wanted desperately not to be thought of as old-fashioned, and during his regime at the National he was frequently accused of being too susceptible to fancy new ideas.

Olivier, then, has always used his performances in and sponsorship of contemporary plays to refresh his classical style. Although he was often eager to balance his work in classical repertory with appearances in commercial West End dramas, he was not interested at first in extending his experience with popular material by acting in films. Throughout the 1930s, as he was developing his skills in Shakespeare and in modern plays, he agreed reluctantly to appear in a number of minor formula films. He hated the work. "Acting in films is about as satisfying as looking at a Michelangelo fresco with a microscope," he scoffed at the time.[14]

On Screen

In his early films, Olivier showed no gifts at all as a movie personality. In conventional entertainments like *The Yellow Ticket* and *Perfect Understanding* (1933), he is handsome but callow. His first Shakespearean performance on film, in *As You Like It* in 1936, is equally unripe. The novice actor does not know how to move in front of the camera, and his voice, though beautifully modulated, is curiously inexpressive. He shakes his head whenever he speaks, and his body movements are stiff. Olivier didn't learn how to "behave" in films until he was directed by William Wyler in *Wuthering Heights* in 1939; and from that point on, he began to respect films and to appreciate the possibilities that the medium offered for the actor. Before working with Wyler he had been convinced that an actor "has no creative part, whatever, in pictures. . . he has no opportunity to build up and exploit a character. He is merely set before a camera and asked to play a short scene."[15]

Although theater historians often dismiss or minimize Olivier's film performances, he in fact developed into a superb film actor. Learning to subdue his titanic energy for the camera, he rarely looked like an illustrious stage actor uncomfortably transporting a proscenium technique to an alien medium. Unlike other eminent stage actors of his generation—John Gielgud, Ralph Richardson, Michael Redgrave, Alec Guinness—Olivier looked like a movie star, and like Richard Burton of a later era, he had the clear-cut choice of

The budding matinee idol, with Gloria Swanson in *Perfect Understanding* (1933).

becoming either a matinee idol or a distinguished classical actor. Olivier, of course, resisted becoming a motion-picture celebrity or a Hollywood personality, but he has never stopped acting in films and his achievement is considerable. Since *Wuthering Heights*, almost every film he has worked on has had impressive credentials. Most have been adaptations of important plays and novels.

Olivier studiously avoided movie-star material that depended solely on presence or charm. As in his theater work, he tried to disguise himself beneath the mask of the character he was playing. He did not want film audiences to identify him as a "personality," and he discouraged the kind of star-audience relationship that sustained the careers of film actors like Clark Gable or Humphrey Bogart or Gary Cooper. Choosing a variety of types of characters, and often playing unsympathetic parts, Olivier resisted developing the strong, distinctive, unchanging persona of the archetypal Hollywood star.

From moony matinee idol to larger-than-life Shakespearean hero to experimental character actor, from *Wuthering Heights* to *Pride and Prejudice* (1940), from *Henry V* (1945) to *Richard III* (1955), from *The Entertainer* (1959) to *Sleuth* (1972) Olivier's work in films is consistently inventive. Film acting did not come naturally to him; he had to work hard to pare away his delight in "business" and movement, to tone down the vocal exaggerations and the outsized vitality that he could get away with in the theater. Kenneth Tynan observed that Olivier is seldom at "the height of his talent" on film "partly because the reticence of movie acting is awkward for him, but mostly because his performances need to be seen as flowing, consecutive entities, not chopped up into close-ups and long-shots spread over months of shooting. You cannot make love by instalments, and Olivier's relationship with his audience is that of a skilled, but dominating lover."[16]

Olivier does not have the total freedom in films that he claims on stage, and as a result he cannot control film audiences to the extent that he can dominate theatergoers. On film, he cannot be as manipulative or, finally, as mesmerizing, as in the theater. "If you succeed in the initial moments of a performance on stage," Olivier has said, "either by a very strong stamp of characterization so they recognize you as a real guy, or by a quiet approach, then I think there's no end to where you can lead them in size of acting a little later in the evening."[17] It is part of the communal nature of the filmmaking process to deny the actor this kind of absolute authority and power. But on film Olivier is a different rather than a diminished performer; he is subtler, more lifelike, and yet his film acting contains echoes of the glorious theatrical thunder. Olivier on film provides a permanent, distinguished record of the evolution of the world's preeminent actor.

2

Early Films

WITH HIS CHISELED PROFILE, his thin, sensual mouth and glowering eyes, his mellow voice, and his tall, trim build, the young Olivier looked like a romantic hero. But on film in the 1930s he was too callow and boyish to offer serious competition to Douglas Fairbanks or Ronald Colman; he was too hesitant to be convincing as a conventional movie hero. Neither claiming film space for himself nor knowing how to yield it to others, Olivier is unresponsive and vague, and there is none of the joy in performance that radiates from the mature actor: Does any other great actor have a comparable record of neophyte incompetence?

Recognizing the young actor's insecurity, producers cast him in the role of an inexperienced, boyish hero who needs an older woman to educate him. Olivier in this period played opposite established actresses who were more knowing than he and who taught him how to "behave like a man." Ann Harding in *Westward Passage* (1931), Lili Damita in *Friends and Lovers* (1931), Elissa Landi in *The Yellow Ticket*, Gloria Swanson in *Perfect Understanding,* and Gertrude Lawrence in *No Funny Business* (1933) scold, coddle, supervise, and pacify the untried young actor. In *As You Like It*, Elisabeth Bergner instructs him in romantic matters, and Flora Robson as Queen Elizabeth mothers him in *Fire Over England* (1937).

The archetypal early Olivier in *The Yellow Ticket* is a naive journalist who wanders wide-eyed through Russia until a persecuted Russian Jew (Elissa Landi) shows him the truth about her country. "I'll bet there's a lot you haven't seen," she informs her handsome, gullible costar. "You've seen what the Russians want you to see." Olivier is pliant, eager to learn: "Could you tell me about Russia?" he asks modestly, "the whole truth about it?"

Laurence Olivier as Heathcliff with Merle Oberon as Cathy on Penistone Crag in Samuel Goldwyn's Wuthering Heights *(1939).*

Olivier is pleasant in this role, but very lightweight. His character's transformation is pushed aside in order to make room for the heroine's encounters with the sinister Baron Andrey, the head of the Czarist secret police (played with wild enthusiasm by Lionel Barrymore). To counteract Olivier's blandness, director Raoul Walsh allowed Barrymore to overact. "I'm not that repulsive," he sputters drunkenly, his eyes popping, as he moves in threateningly on the horror-struck heroine. Although Barrymore's muttered, extravagantly mannered performance is an anthology of ham-acting techniques, his blatant and self-parodying exhibitionism supplies the color so lacking in Olivier's anemic delivery: the film needs Barrymore as insurance against Olivier!

The Yellow Ticket is representative of Olivier's earliest film work, but even later in the decade, after he had played Romeo, Hamlet, and Iago on stage, he had still not acquired an authoritative presence on film. In neither of the two films he made with Vivien Leigh in 1937, *Fire Over England* and *Twenty-One Days Together*, does he suggest promise: the unusual and striking Shakespearean stage actor remained unpersuasive on film.

In *Fire Over England*, Olivier and Leigh provide the secondary love interest to a highly patriotic version of the defeat of the Spanish Armada: the film was intended as a reminder to Hitler of England's tenacious resistance to foreign invasion. Flora Robson's matronly, benevolent Queen Elizabeth is fond of the juvenile leads: "She is a minx; and he is so tall!" "You are yesterday," she chides the loyal Leicester, "and *he* is tomorrow," she says, pointing with a proprietary air to the swashbuckling hero played by Olivier. The queen instructs Olivier in how to save England from Spanish conquest. As his country's savior, Olivier leaps on and off ships and balconies; engages in brisk swordplay; courts an aristocratic Spanish lady in addition to making love to Vivien Leigh's lady-in-waiting; masquerades as a spy in the Spanish court; and sings a song about wooing. The character is almost never seen in repose. Olivier, however, doesn't have the graceful exuberance of Fairbanks or the easy charm of Errol Flynn that the material needs. Many times throughout the action, after he's completed a daring mission or while he's receiving counsel from the queen, his character must kneel, and Olivier slumps down on one knee as he scowls in evident discontent. "Not again, surely?" he seems to be saying to himself.

Nonetheless this was Olivier's most generous film role to date, for in addition to the athletic feats, he is given a big dramatic scene in which he weeps for his father's death and rages against the Spaniards who killed him. At the time Olivier didn't have the zest and abandon that would properly decorate this popular historical romance, but there are fleeting glimpses of power; his voice for the first time on film has dark undertones as well as lyrical highlights; and he plays responsively with Vivien Leigh, who is charming as a saucy court attendant, and with Flora Robson as the wise queen.

Olivier and Leigh are, finally, agreeable amateurs in *Fire Over England*, but in *Twenty-One Days Together* they are both remarkably pale. Graham Greene's screenplay, based on a short story by John Galsworthy, establishes a contrast between two brothers, a ne'er-do-well (Olivier) and an eminent judge (Leslie Banks). Like the Surface brothers in *School for Scandal*, the "good" brother turns out to be a hypocrite and the "bad" brother reveals moral strength. The film creates a sinister atmosphere of squalid boardinghouses and crowded streets and pubs in which Olivier and Leigh, bland and well scrubbed, look altogether out of place. She is arch, distant, practically unrecognizable; he is blurred and superficial.

They have a scene in a sunny restaurant that should be played charmingly. Olivier begins the scene by knocking over a vase of flowers, and his acting is so clumsy that it is impossible to tell if the spill is a deliberate part of his characterization or a mistake that hasn't been edited out. Olivier is altogether too solemn and tongue-tied, and too bumbling, to play the jaunty world adventurer that the script asks for.

Twenty-One Days Together wasn't released until after the success of *Gone With the Wind* and *Wuthering Heights*, and it was quite an embarrassment to both actors. While they were appearing on Broadway in their unsuccessful *Romeo and Juliet* in 1940, they went to see the film and were shocked by these earlier, unfinished versions of themselves. Olivier asked friends not to see it: "We had to do a remake of it to make it good enough to put on the shelf," he said.[1]

Not yet a character actor and certainly not a spectacularly scaled personality in his own right, the young Olivier had very little to offer movies except for a pleasing voice and appearance. Olivier didn't respect films, and his contempt poisons his performances. Because he regarded film acting as slumming for money, he was reluctant to accept a part in the one serious film project that was offered to him

during this period. Impressed by Olivier's unconventional performance in Gielgud's production of *Romeo and Juliet*, Paul Czinner
asked him to play Orlando in his film adaptation of *As You Like It*.
Olivier was suspicious of acting Shakespeare on film, and he thought
the play itself would be swamped by the realistic production Czinner was planning. He also felt that the camera's demand for realism
would make the Elizabethan stage convention of the heroine disguised as a boy look foolish (in Shakespeare's time, the disguise took
on Pirandellian overtones because a boy was playing a girl disguised
as a boy). Olivier's skepticism was justified, as it turned out, for *As
You Like It* is unsatisfactory Shakespeare and uncertain filmmaking,
and Olivier's own performance is barely competent.

Orlando is the least-challenging Shakespearean character Olivier
has ever played, but at the time, in 1936, he had a gangling, boyish
quality that suited him for the role. His Orlando, in fact, looks like
another of his romantic leading-man parts in which he is manipu-
lated by a clever older woman. An idealized romantic figure who
defeats the duke's champion wrestler, saves his evil brother from
death, and falls in love with a princess who tests his sincerity, Orlando is the kind of standard hero that the mature Olivier avoided
playing. There is no opportunity for Orlando to woo the audience or
to dominate the action, and it isn't surprising that Olivier is confined
to being simply handsome and well spoken. Since the character is
dominated by Rosalind, one of Shakespeare's bossiest heroines, the
actor playing Orlando needs a strong, vigorous actress to react to.
Elisabeth Bergner, however, turns Shakespeare's keen, resourceful, controlling heroine into mush. Bergner makes Rosalind impos-
sibly coy and sweet where the character should be firm and unsentimental. She reduces Shakespeare's shrewd mistress of the revels
to a collection of gamine mannerisms, and her ugly Germanic accent
completely destroys the wit and melody of the verse. Her impossi-
bly self-centered acting pushes Olivier into himself, so that the two
of them never seem to be occupying the same film space.

Working on *As You Like It* was nonetheless valuable experience
for Olivier since he remembered Czinner's wrong decisions when
he directed his own film adaptations of the Bard. In *As You Like It*,
settings reinforce theme: the court is opposed to the forest in the
play's moral scheme, and this contrast certainly invites the creation
of the kind of concrete physical reality that is the natural property of
film. But Czinner doesn't find a visual concept that matches the

spirit of the language. This is one of Shakespeare's airiest comedies, yet the film's court setting is massive and ponderous, looking as if it belongs in an epic rather than a lyrical comedy; and the Forest of Arden is presented as a perplexing mixture of artifice and reality. Real sheep are paraded against fake fauna and a studio sky, and the brooks and trees and hillocks belong to the back lot rather than to nature. Space in this forest is studio-created and cramped, yet real animals move through it. Czinner even includes a scene of altogether-misplaced realism in which a snake coils around Orlando's evil brother while a lion crouches in readiness for attack. This sudden image of nature as predatory is jarring, and it darkens the story in a way Shakespeare had not intended.

Shakespeare's poetry, in the unlocalized Elizabethan stage setting, did the work of the scenic designer—the Forest of Arden was created through language rather than props. But on film, the space has to be filled—a tangible world has to be created—and Czinner's forest never looks plentiful and verdant enough; it doesn't look capable of magically transforming all those who enter it. In this forest, after all, lovers are united, brothers are reconciled, the state is healed, the wicked grow benevolent. The film's Arden hasn't the proper look of enchantment.

In his skeptical review of the film, Graham Greene chastised the filmmaker for his misguided concern for realism and for his unimaginative use of the camera: "[Czinner] seems to have concluded that all the cinema can offer is more space: more elaborate palace sets and a real wood with room for real animals. How the ubiquitous livestock (sheep and cows and hens and rabbits) weary us before the end, and how disastrously the genuine English woodland is spoilt by too much fancy, for when did English trees, in what is apparently late autumn, bear clusters of white flowers? Freedom of movement, too, is often misused, and why should poetry be cut merely to leave time for girlish games of touch-wood through the trees? On only one occasion is the camera a definite gain. The lyrical repetitions between Sylvius and Phebe, Orlando and Rosalind: 'It is to be all made of sighs and tears: And so am I for Phebe.' 'And I for Ganymede.' 'And I for Rosalind.' 'And I for no Woman,' with the help of of the rhythmically panning camera move beautifully into the memory."[2]

The film's inconsistent visual style, neither frankly theatrical nor seriously realistic, is a hindrance to the actors who are thus trapped against settings that are either inappropriately heavy or unintentionally fake. Having learned from Czinner's mistakes, Olivier in his own adaptations softened the clash between Shakespeare's theatricality and the inherent realism of films.

Wuthering Heights, three years later, was the actor's first great popular success in the movies, and it gave him the kind of acclaim that he had sought when he tried out for the ill-fated *Beau Geste* a decade earlier. For the first time, he looked comfortable on film; the sensuality and emotional power that had been struggling for expression in the earlier formula films were finally released. *Wuthering Heights* made Olivier a movie star, and he could have had a glamorous film career. Because, however, he chose the challenge of great classical roles rather than an easy success that traded on his appearance and manner, Olivier's tenure as a full-fledged Hollywood star is surprisingly brief. In addition to *Wuthering Heights*, his romantic roles include only Maxim de Winter in *Rebecca* (1940), Darcy in *Pride and Prejudice*, and Admiral Nelson in *That Hamilton Woman* (1941). Less than two years after his successful Heathcliff, Olivier walked away from a glossy film career; he refused to allow fame and acclamation to limit or corrupt his development as an actor. He knew that at the time he was unfinished as a performer and that the best place to develop would be in classical repertory rather than in formulaic movie romances.

Even the roles he selected as follow-ups to Heathcliff, however, when he was the most sought-after actor in Hollywood, had temperament and individuality. Determined to transcend stereotype, he chose heroes who were in some way flawed or unacceptable, whose appeal, in fact, was based on some character defect. The dark, romantic Olivier hero was rigid, ironic, sinister; there was something threatening and almost otherworldly about him, and he seemed to belong in a particularly neurotic Gothic novel. Even in his brief matinee-idol phase, then, Olivier avoided being merely charming or urbane; he was instead the isolated hero, the wounded prince, the man with a secret obsession. In his four high romances, he plays a worldly, powerful man (these roles offer an interesting, and decisive, shift from his earlier image as an innocent) who is too proud for his own well-being. As Heathcliff, as Maxim de Winter, as Darcy, and (to a lesser extent) as Admiral Nelson, Olivier plays a magnetic outsider, a troubled and bewitching stranger rather than a conventional man of action.

With his dramatic transformation, his dark sexuality, and his elemental rage, Emily Brontë's Heathcliff is an ideal role for the young, ambitious actor. Heathcliff is one of the great outsiders in English literature, but the filmmakers were afraid of him, and they turned Brontë's driven character into a much less threatening figure than he is in the novel. Ben Hecht and Charles MacArthur's screenplay reduces the character to a lovesick stable boy who is brooding and quixotic but who lacks the titanic rage, the lust for revenge, of the great tortured original. Brontë's hero is impelled by an ecstatic passion; at home on the moors and in the world of violent, untamed nature that encloses Wuthering Heights, he is a divine primitive. Samuel Goldwyn's big-budget Hollywood film doesn't have the vocabulary to encompass Heathcliff as Brontë wrote him, and it tamed him, thereby limiting Olivier's possibilities.

Enthusiastic for the first time about a film role, Olivier wanted to put on a lot of makeup for Heathcliff; he wanted to play him in the early scenes as dirty and wild, but Goldwyn thought a smudged Olivier would offend the audience. So the film presents a Heathcliff that is scrubbed from the beginning, whereas in the novel the character is respectably groomed only after he leaves Wuthering Heights and has been transformed by his experiences in the world beyond the moors. The new Heathcliff returns a proper gentleman, and as such provides a startling contrast to the unschooled foundling who lived among the animals and was at peace only on the moors.

Denied the use of makeup, Olivier tries to suggest the heathenish quality of the character through movement, and as the wretched, put-upon stable boy he has a shuffling walk and a hunched, tensed posture that points a contrast to the assured and expansive Heathcliff who returns from the outside world. Olivier also uses his eyes—accusing, scornful, glowering—to deepen the characterization.

The film civilizes the relationship between Heathcliff and Cathy. The scenes of their childhood romance and their deep attachment as young lovers are few and they lack the intensity and radiance, the almost subversive, antisocial energy, that drive Brontë's originals. Hecht and MacArthur emphasize Cathy's schoolgirl romanticism; she imagines Heathcliff as a foreign prince, and she pretends that Penistone Crag is their castle. The fairy-tale motif of the questing knight who rescues the sleeping princess is only dimly present in the novel, and its use here is intended to normalize the lovers. The film also stresses Cathy's interest in society. The film's heroine is more enticed than Brontë's character by the worldliness of Thrushcross Grange; this Cathy yearns almost as much for respectability as she does for the moors. Cathy berates Heathcliff for his unmannerliness, and the film seems to suggest that if only he had been as inclined as Cathy to bourgeois comforts, their separation could have been avoided. The characters are made to conform, then, to an archetypal Hollywood story of the lady and the peasant, and the grand eccentrics, the isolated, transfixed characters of the novel, are therefore considerably diminished: this version of the story is a melodrama of mistiming rather than a tragedy of a consuming passion.

The screenwriters confronted the problems of adaptation by cutting the book in half. Although eliminating the children (Cathy, Hareton, and Linton) makes commercial sense since the second-generation story would prolong the film unduly as well as diminish the star parts, the children's history raises Cathy and Heathcliff to mythic heights and gives their passion a universal significance. Further, omitting the children softens Heathcliff's character since it is in the second half of the novel that he is truly satanic. His own entangled feelings of love and hate are expressed through his ruthless domination of the children; forcing the marriage between Linton and Cathy, acting out his revenge for Hindley on Hareton, disgusted by Linton's weakness, enchanted and finally saved by Cathy's resemblance to her mother, Heathcliff becomes a doomed, haunted man who moves like a hulking devil through Wuthering Heights. Eliminating this obsessed character who wills his own death deprives Olivier of playing a full-scale Heathcliff. The film reserves Cathy's deathbed scene for Heathcliff's most impassioned moment, thereby enforcing our sense of the character as a heartbroken lover rather than a crazed tyrant overwhelmed by his feelings for his dead mistress.

Given the film's sentimentalized concept, it was impossible for Olivier to act a majestically sinister Heathcliff. Although an authentic rendering of Brontë's character may have been beyond his powers at the time, we can still feel him chafing against the limited, contained character he has been forced to play. The film's Heathcliff is too civilized right from the start, though Olivier hints at the tempestuous feelings that drive Brontë's original character and there are isolated moments where his concept of Heathcliff almost

matches Brontë's. The film retains the prologue, in which
Lockwood, the new tenant at the Grange, calls at Wuthering
Heights during a snowstorm. Lockwood finds a tyrannical, dour
Heathcliff, a man eaten away by years of bitterness; and in these first
moments Olivier plays the maddened character in a way that
suggests the Heathcliff that broods over the second part of the
novel. His interpretation in the film's opening moments must carry
the burden of many pages of exposition; he must create an image
that will stay with us for the rest of the film. It is appropriate,
therefore, that his performance in these early scenes is especially
intense. After Lockwood reports that he has seen a woman outside
the bedroom window, Olivier throws him from the room in a rage
and then rushes out into the blizzard, screaming for his beloved
Cathy. It is an operatic moment, and only in two other scenes is
Olivier as forceful. When he tells Isabella that he cannot stand her,
he is chilling; and in the climactic deathbed scene, he is immensely
moving. When he berates Cathy for squandering their love by mar-
rying the worldly, pale Edgar and when, after she dies, he prays for
her spirit to haunt him, he acts with a grandeur that transcends the
film's popular-romance gentility.

Though for the most part Olivier is too reserved and proper,
though the film denies him the tragic heights the part contains, his
Heathcliff was his first accomplished work in films, his first film
performance that contains intimations of greatness. There are sub-
tleties in his characterization designed for the close-up camera that
could never register on the stage: his silent anger as he holds his
hands for Hindley to mount a horse; his intensely sensual scrutiny of
Cathy in the ball at Thrushcross Grange. He is disappointing in
some important scenes, however. The lovers' meetings on Penistone Crag establish their special bond, but Olivier's awkwardness in
these scenes recalls his unhappy days as a film novice. And in the
crucial scene in which Heathcliff is ordered out of Thrushcross
Grange—a moment that the vengeful character will nurse for the
rest of his life—Olivier doesn't pronounce his promise of revenge
with the elemental fury that ought to be there. His denunciation of
the very civilized Linton family is surprisingly casual.

Olivier's characterization is not enhanced by Merle Oberon's
ladylike Cathy. While Oberon plays strongly within the film's circumscribed concept of the character, her demure Cathy, who seems
entirely content with a conventional, enclosed life with Edgar Lin-

ton, inevitably reduces the scope of Olivier's Heathcliff. Oberon performs to the limits of her capacities; her impassioned "I *am* Heathcliff!" announced against a clap of lightning and thunder; her heated arguments with Isabella; her high-handedness with Heathcliff; and her deathbed scene are all intelligent and moving. Oberon is appropriate for this mass-market version of *Wuthering Heights*, whereas Geraldine Fitzgerald, as Isabella, almost dismantles it, since she unleashes a Brontë-esque intensity and rage that the movie has worked so studiously to suppress. She alone suggests the heightened feelings that propel Brontë's characters to their catastrophic fates. Fitzgerald has only a few scenes, in which she makes us believe utterly in her passion for Heathcliff. Her character seems demonically possessed. If Goldwyn had thought she was pretty enough to play Cathy, and if Olivier had been allowed to charge through his role at full force, this would have been an ecstatic interpretation of *Wuthering Heights* rather than one that is too well-bred.

For Olivier, the film was a real turning point. He had accepted the part very reluctantly, convinced at the time that the filmmaking process frustrated the work of serious actors, but during the course of filming he found to his surprise that he enjoyed the way films are pieced together and he began to think for the first time about directing a film himself. Olivier has always credited William Wyler, who directed *Wuthering Heights*, for teaching him most of what he knows about acting for the movies.

But Olivier was anxious about returning to Hollywood for personal as well as theoretical reasons: on his last visit, in 1933, he had been fired as Greta Garbo's leading man in *Queen Christina*. Garbo, ice maiden and prima donna, was unresponsive to him on the set, apparently because she wanted her friend John Gilbert to have the role; the career of the silent-film actor was on the decline because his voice did not record well, and Garbo wanted him to have another chance. At the time of his dismissal, Olivier felt he had been ill-used, and he left the movie colony vowing never to return. In retrospect, Olivier gallantly says that he was fired because he was too much of a lightweight to hold the screen with the magnetic Garbo; he feels that, in 1933, he was really too callow and inexperienced, too unprepossessing, to have been effective opposite her.

Wyler was the first director to develop Olivier's skill as a film actor. Their relationship was not an easy one, however. By 1938, after his notorious Romeo and his unorthodox performances at the Old Vic, Olivier had much more confidence than when he had been overshadowed by Garbo. He now had a sense of himself as a seasoned classical actor, and he brought to his preliminary readings of Heathcliff a rhetorical heightening inappropriate for the greater realism and the more intimate scale required of film-acting. Wyler, therefore, had to tone him down, to erase the too-florid theatrical flourishes. There were also problems because Wyler is among the most inarticulate of good directors; he does not tell actors what he wants from them but commands them instead to perform single takes over and over again until they discover exactly the "right" qualities in the scene. Along with his colleagues, Olivier caviled at Wyler's repeated injunctions to "do it again!" How could they correct what was wrong if they weren't given any concrete instructions? To Olivier, strictly trained in classical technique, Wyler's approach was maddeningly vague: Olivier could not understand this method of acting by osmosis. Yet Wyler's unorthodox and exasperating style has resulted in performances of uniform excellence in his films. Though Olivier was never able to say exactly how it had happened, he realized that Wyler had slyly coaxed him into delivering a beautifully attuned film performance, one that remains among his most effective in the medium. Olivier knew he had real power as Heathcliff, and he knew that his director had helped him to release it and to adjust it for the camera.

Five years later, when he was offered the opportunity to direct *Henry V* for films, Olivier at first declined because he felt he knew too little about filmmaking. He asked Wyler to direct, thereby acknowledging both the respect and the sense of indebtedness he felt for his film mentor. Wyler turned down the offer because he felt that he didn't know enough about Shakespeare, and at the same time he encouraged Olivier to go ahead with the project because he was confident that Olivier did in fact know enough about films.

After working with Wyler, Olivier was coached in his next film by Alfred Hitchcock, another director whose methods were antagonistic to his own training and instinct and who has been widely quoted as claiming that actors are "cattle." As with every public pronouncement he made, this one too was sly and deceptive: Hitchcock did and did not mean it. Often, Hitchcock obtained superior performances from normally indifferent actors, but he was not an actor's director, and his actors, of course, were never allowed to up-

stage him. A film signed by Hitchcock is one that has been
thoroughly controlled by him. His actors, as part of his precon-
ceived master plan, are made to follow orders. Characters in Hitchcock films are often trapped in a deterministic world where the
notion of free will is impossible, irrelevant, or laughed at. Hitchcock
exercised the same kind of control over his actors, who are kept
firmly in place. Bravura moments in Hitchcock belong not to the
performers but to the director as he displays his masterly creation of
mood and atmosphere, his skillful cross-cutting, his apt placement
of the camera, his cleverness in building (and breaking) tension.

Olivier and Joan Fontaine with director Alfred Hitchcock on the set of *Rebecca*
(1940).

Moving from Wyler's vague, repetitive methods to Hitchcock's stringent commands, Olivier was forced into becoming a disciplined film actor. After his strenuous workouts with these two temperamental directors, he had adjusted to the fact that the director was the true "author" of a film, and he had grown used to the fragmentation of film acting. He had even begun to enjoy the process by which a film performance is built: the bits and pieces, the takes and retakes, filmed out of sequence, which are then assembled at the mercy of the editor. He had begun to accept the comparative lack of control that the actor has over his own performance.

For his third assignment in this "high" Hollywood phase of his career, as Darcy in *Pride and Prejudice,* Olivier worked in a much more relaxed atmosphere. His director, Robert Z. Leonard, was a competent studio craftsman, with none of the perfectionist zeal or the autocratic personal temperament of either Wyler or Hitchcock. Leonard did not impose himself on his films or his actors; he was not the kind of director who was drawn over and over again to the same themes and character types. He worked on a variety of different subjects, doing ably and reliably what his studio, Metro-Goldwyn-Mayer, assigned him to do. If Olivier had made *Pride and Prejudice* first, before his movie apprenticeship with Wyler and Hitchcock, the results might well have been unfortunate; but after he had been instructed by two masters in the fine points of behaving in front of a camera, he could create his characterization of Darcy with only minimal assistance from Leonard. Olivier's performance in the film, in fact, has the ease and subtlety of a practiced film actor.

In *Rebecca, Pride and Prejudice,* and *That Hamilton Woman,* Olivier plays dashing, ambiguous, aloof characters whose charm is shadowed by melancholy and a biting wit. All three characters are capable of startling explosions of anger and cynicism; all three are scowling autocrats who are neither warm-hearted nor easily likable. They are moody, surly, disfigured either emotionally or physically: as he developed confidence and style as a film performer, Olivier selected characters who are darker, more intense and complicated, than the suave Ronald Colman parts that by age and appearance he was certainly qualified to play.

Like Heathcliff, Olivier's Maxim de Winter in *Rebecca* is a romantic outsider, a man of special feeling who is isolated from the world. Brooding and solitary, Maxim rules Manderley, his family

estate, the same way that the haunted Heathcliff controlled
Wuthering Heights. Daphne Du Maurier's character does not, of
course, have the grandeur of Brontë's dark protagonist, but Olivier
plays his Gothic hero with the same capacity for rage that he gave
Heathcliff. His explosions in *Rebecca* have a Shakespearean intensity that makes Du Maurier's story seem more dense and intriguing
than it really is.

For most of the film, we're encouraged to regard Maxim as a man
in mourning for his beloved wife, Rebecca. From our first view of
him, standing on a cliff, we are teased into thinking of him as suici-
dal, and we read his distracted manner and his sudden explosions as
signs of romantic despair. Until the long-delayed exposition, in
which he reveals that Rebecca was "incapable of love or decency"
and that he feels responsible for her death even though he did not in
fact kill her, we have been prodded to see him as a selfish, dangerous man in love with his own grief. Our sympathy has been directed
to the meek second Mrs. de Winter (Joan Fontaine), whom he treats
callously. We never know more than she does about the tortured
master of Manderley, and so we react to him as she does, with
growing discomfort and suspicion.

Maxim is a richly ambiguous role, then, which affords Olivier the
chance to play a kind of hide-and-seek game with the audience. He
encourages us to see the character in double focus, as both debonair
and sinister, as a man of the world who yet seems capable of murder. Joan Fontaine says to him early in their relationship, "You're
not an easy subject to sketch. . .your expression keeps changing all
the time." He's a broken man, but he's capable of being fatherly to
his insecure new wife and he is a great romantic who indulges in
self-pity: "It's over now, our chance for happiness. Rebecca has
won, her shadow has been between us all the time. . . . I've known
all along that Rebecca would win in the end."

It is exactly this unsettled quality of the character, with its rapid
alternations between tenderness and sarcasm, its venomous outbursts, its darting implications of evil, that creates the main narrative tension. Because of what Olivier suggests that Maxim might be
capable of, we are afraid for his wife.

Olivier's eruptions provide dramatic highlights throughout the
film. "What the devil are you shouting at?" he demands of Joan
Fontaine the first time he sees her, when she tries to warn him of
danger at the edge of the cliff. "Who are you? What are you staring

at?" After they're married, he treats his new wife like a misbehaving child or an intruder, berating her for innocent mistakes. "I sometimes seem to fly off the handle for no reason at all, don't I?" he asks by way of half-hearted apology. "I'm afraid I've become boorish through living alone." When, unknowingly, she dresses up in Rebecca's clothes for a costume ball, he bellows at her mercilessly.

Since Hitchcock does not permit his actors to have more space than is absolutely necessary for story purposes, Olivier is not allowed to dominate the film. Hitchcock keeps him in line, especially in his restrained confession scene; at times, Olivier seems like a puppet responding on cue to Hitchcock's calculated master plan. But Hitchcock has been uncharacteristically generous to Judith Anderson, who plays Rebecca's fanatically loyal servant, Mrs. Danvers. With its startling suggestions of perversity ("Sometimes I wonder if Rebecca doesn't come back and watch you and Mr. de Winter together"), its sepulchral intonations and grande-dame hauteur, her performance has all the signs of bravura classical acting in comparison to which Olivier seems positively self-effacing. Anderson's sly, high-camp performance comes as close to upstaging Hitchcock as any of his actors ever has.

Olivier's Darcy in *Pride and Prejudice* is even more subdued than his Maxim de Winter in *Rebecca*. Once again, he plays a character who appears to be other than what he really is. Beneath his haughty mask, Darcy turns out to be generous and loyal. By hinting throughout the action at the softer character that underlies the intimidating surface, Olivier presents Jane Austen's hero as a round rather than a flat comic character. "Your arrogance, your conceit, your selfish disregard of other people's feelings made me dislike you from the first," Elizabeth Bennett (Greer Garson) chastises him when he proposes to her. "It is I who should be ashamed—of my arrogance, my stupid pride, of all my faults—except I am not ashamed of having loved you," Darcy humbly offers in his speech of reformation. Both sides of the character—the unlikable prig and the yielding gentleman—are accounted for in Olivier's subtle interpretation.

Avoiding comedy-of-manners caricature, Olivier plays Darcy, then, as a fully developed character, thereby being faithful to the design of the novel in which only Darcy and Elizabeth change and mature while the supporting characters are comic masks. Olivier's proud Darcy and Greer Garson's prejudiced Elizabeth learn from their clashing encounters, their too-hasty judgments of each other, and they help each other to become wise. As in the novel, these reluctant lovers remain detached from the other characters (who are sketched in with a few prominent traits) by being more sober and complex; and yet they enact their characters' moral reformation without violating Jane Austen's trenchant comic tone, her superb irony. In the proposal scene, for instance, Olivier and Garson discover a pathos that expands the characters without discounting Austen's objective, comic view of the scene. Olivier is hesitant, repressed, formal, yet a gentleman of true feeling nonetheless. Tenderly he whispers "I love you" to Elizabeth, but his pride and his sharp tongue are in evidence, too: "Do you expect me to be glad that your family is inferior to mine?" he asks waspishly. After Elizabeth rejects him, he mournfully announces that "this is perhaps the last time I shall see you. God bless you, Elizabeth." The farewell is so moving that for a moment Olivier risks turning *Pride and Prejudice* into a sentimental drama.

From the rejection until the reformed lovers are finally united, Olivier gives us a double view of the character as Darcy's formal social manner, his icy decorum, imperfectly conceal his wounded feelings. Darcy's longing gazes at Elizabeth introduce an autumnal note into Jane Austen's bright comedy, but Olivier doesn't neglect the character's stinging sarcasm. "I'm in no humor tonight to give consequences to the middle classes at play," he sneers during the ball. "Isn't it exquisitely funny, Mr. Darcy?" a snobbish friend asks him, referring to the Bennett family's social disgrace when one of their daughters runs off with a soldier. "Exquisitely; just think how you would roar with laughter if it happened to yourself," he replies in a tone of quietly devastating irony.

Olivier's mellifluous voice and courtly manner are ideally suited to Jane Austen. Playing an aristocratic gentleman of leisure, he uses fussy, elegant gestures, adjusting his vest, lightly tapping his nose and face to emphasize key words, bowing decorously, while remaining manly and self-contained.

Greer Garson's arch but warm-hearted Elizabeth is equally faithful to the spirit of Jane Austen, and she too does some neat work with period details, with fans and flounces, to amplify her character. The screenplay by Aldous Huxley and Jane Murfin preserves Austen's dialogue, with its graceful, periodic sentences, its use of elaborate parallel structure, its epigrammatic wit, and it economically condenses the action without sacrificing any major characters or incidents. But for all the charm of its performers and the skill of its construction, the film cannot duplicate the experience of reading the novel, for two elements crucial to Jane Austen's art are missing: duration, and the alert, droll presence of the author herself. Jane Austen explores Elizabeth's changing feelings for Darcy with a richness of detail, of psychological discriminations, that the film—any film—cannot hope to match. Elizabeth's consciousness is the center of the novel, whereas in the film what Elizabeth thinks and says and does must compete with the sets and the costumes and the necessity for moving ahead briskly with the story. The filmmakers don't have enough time to let us savor the character's thoughts fully, and they simply don't have the kind of access to Elizabeth that Jane Austen has: the film is an external presentation of material that is presented in the novel as part of the heroine's internal thoughts, her complex shifts of attitude and feeling and perception: we never know Greer Garson's Elizabeth as intimately as we know the novel's enchanting, devious, complex heroine.

Olivier has a much easier role, since even in the novel Darcy is seen in long shot, from the outside. Because Darcy is a character who is perceived rather than one, like Elizabeth, who actively perceives, he is more easily transferrable to film. Intelligent as she is in the part, Greer Garson is not the great friend that the novel's heroine becomes to us, while Olivier in a more superficial role is closer to our experience of Darcy while reading Austen.

Though he has tried carefully to retain Jane Austen's characteristic tone in the dialogue, Huxley could not find a point of view that corresponds to the novelist's function in her own story. Jane Austen is the controlling presence in *Pride and Prejudice*, for it is she who watches over the characters in varying degrees of disapproval, and it is her wonderfully dry point of view, her superbly poised objectivity, that guide us through the story, drolly commenting on her character even while we are being told, in intimate detail, what Elizabeth is thinking. In the novel, we are both inside and outside the character, and this double view is part of the deliciously ironic texture of Austen's writing. Without Jane Austen's authorial voice—and any film version of her work must inevitably be without it, even if the filmmakers added a voiceover narration that was bound to be strained and artificial—this version of *Pride and Prej-udice* is only a skeletal rendition of the inimitable original.

That Hamilton Woman: Korda and the Oliviers

The Hollywood phase of Olivier's film career was shortlived for a number of reasons. By the time he had achieved international fame in *Wuthering Heights*, Olivier was already seriously committed to the classics and to continuing to measure himself against the great tradition in British acting. Film work, no matter how much he came to respect it, could be seen only as a series of departures from that goal. So even at the height of his movie fame, in 1939 and 1940, Olivier was interested in returning to the theater; indeed, immediately after finishing *Wuthering Heights*, he began planning a production of *Romeo and Juliet* to star himself and Vivien Leigh. Presented on Broadway in 1940, after successful tryout engagements in San Francisco and Chicago, the production was the most spectacular failure of his career. As director, Olivier wanted a meticulously realistic design for the play, a sense of place and of space more suited to the world of physical reality that can best be created on film rather than on stage. Olivier was criticized not only for the overly ornate and visually fussy production, but for his staccato delivery of the verse. He was accused of being frequently unintelligible and of sacrificing the poetry for unnecessary displays of athletic prowess. As in 1935, he was again offering a restless, impetuous, physical, almost manic Romeo who dashed about the stage with the agility of Douglas Fairbanks in *The Thief of Bagdad*. Vivien Leigh was treated only slightly more gently—her voice was too light to carry effectively in the enormous theater, usually reserved for musical comedies, where the production was given.

After their humiliating reception, the actors (now married, and now known everywhere as the Oliviers) were especially eager to return to England. Neither felt temperamentally suited for life in Hollywood (or New York), or for conforming to the demands of a powerful studio. Olivier has always been the architect of his own career, and so the prospect of studio management seemed to him a particularly bothersome intrusion.

When England declared war on Germany, Olivier and other English actors working in Hollywood wanted to return at once to serve their country. They were told to wait, and for the Oliviers, this waiting period was filled with anxiety because they were separated from their children, Olivier's son, Tarquin, and Leigh's daughter, Susannah. Finished for the moment with film commitments, and trying to recover from the failure, late in 1940, of *Romeo and Juliet*, they hoped to return home until Alexander Korda, himself in exile from England, persuaded them to star in his film of *That Hamilton Woman* as a way of serving their country. He presented the film to them on the basis of its propaganda value as a salute to British heroism in an earlier war. Korda believed that the story of Hamilton's defense of Britain against Napoleon offered a pointed parallel to current events, providing a reminder of Britain's valor in repelling invasion. Using his considerable powers of persuasion, he convinced the Oliviers to appear in the film, assuring them that their participation would be a patriotic gesture.

In 1941, though temporarily uprooted by the war, Korda was still the most influential producer in British films. With his production of *The Private Life of Henry VIII*, in 1933, England for the first time became a competitor in the international film market. *Henry VIII*, which is still considered the most profitable British film ever made, was a great success, the first British film to make a serious impact outside native boundaries. In the United States, the film received the popular stamp of approval by opening (and doing well) at Radio City Music Hall. For the first time, Hollywood studios took notice of the fact that the British had a film industry after all.

Throughout the remainder of the 1930s, and for most of the 1940s, Korda was the chief architect of the British film industry, its principal overseer, its chief developer of talent, its kingpin entrepreneur. A cigar-chomping wheeler-dealer, Korda had already had an extraordinary producing career before he almost single-handedly boosted the British industry to a place of international prominence. Korda had had two separate careers by this time, in fact—in his native Hungary, in the 1910s and early 1920s, and in Hollywood in the late 1920s. In both these earlier phases of his peripatetic career, Korda had achieved a high place against great odds. But he did not become a truly international figure until *Henry VIII*, a film made very much to satisfy Korda's personal taste. He had devised the formula of presenting the private lives of legendary figures in a 1928 film, made in Hollywood, called *The Private Life of Helen of Troy*.

Korda had a rich, complex personality. He was a shrewd financier who also aspired to culture and taste. He was a man who could put through deals, though he often made astounding miscalculations. Like the phoenix, he rose from his own ashes. Several times, he built a film empire only to see it crumble because of schemes that were too grandiose and unrealistic; leaping before he looked, he made a series of reckless decisions and he offered moviegoers many films they did not really want to see. Yet after each collapse of his domain, he managed a heroic comeback. No matter how many failures he had, he could always charm influential people into believing in his new plans. He had a more refined manner than the stereotypical Hollywood mogul. With the air of a bon vivant, he knew how to ingratiate himself with the rich and the famous, though at heart he was a loner. In both his private life and his business dealings, he had to be in control, he had to play the tyrant—he "created" Merle Oberon, and then he married her. Capable of great loyalty, he could also be ruthless and unforgiving. And he was wildly self-destructive, eating voraciously against doctors' orders, for instance, and working compulsively at feverish pace, always in search of a new angle and a new production package.

He made the kinds of films that he himself wanted to see, and a film produced by Korda bears the stamp of his personal signature as much as the work of an *auteur* director represents the force and sway of his particular sensibility. Korda's historical romances, exotic adventure sagas, and sophisticated comedies of manners—the three main subject areas in which he specialized—were known for their tasteful production values and for their star actors. Korda had an excellent sense of star potential, and he had under contract most of the major actors of the time. All of the important English actors of the 1930s and 1940s appeared in at least one Korda production. Before *Gone With the Wind*, Vivien Leigh was a Korda contract player, appearing in such lightweight comedies as *Storm in a Teacup* (with Rex Harrison).

Korda was often criticized by other British producers because his films were not distinctly British in tone or subject matter. In the late 1930s and early 1940s, he tried to rectify the charges of being unpatriotic by producing a series of films on British historical subjects; of these, his two with Olivier and Leigh, *Fire Over England* and *That Hamilton Woman*, were the most popular. After the war, when he returned to England, he resumed his production activities, remaining active until his death in 1957, though never again dominating the industry as he had in the 1930s. No longer a trendsetter, he seemed in fact to have distinctly old-fashioned tastes, yet, as always, he withstood a series of commercial and artistic setbacks with remarkable resiliency.

Under Korda's direction, *That Hamilton Woman* was made, then, as a morale-booster for the English. Given the upbeat, patriotic concept, the Oliviers were required to play romanticized versions of their historical characters. The film's official function—its celebration of Nelson's victory over Napoleon—competes with and finally dims the notorious love story between the admiral and Lady Hamilton. Forced to keep a high tone on their characters, Leigh never for a moment suggests Emma Hamilton's background as a courtesan and "specialty" dancer, and Olivier plays Nelson in a conventional manner as a proud military commander and a heroic man in love with a bewitching, though always dignified, woman.

Olivier would have liked to play Nelson as an erratic and egocentric character, but he felt that it was neither the time nor the movie to go beyond a popular idea of a national hero. Despite the fact that Olivier, playing with one arm, graying hair, an eye patch, and a prominent scar, looks made up for a flamboyant character part, his interpretation is surprisingly straightforward.

By this time, he had begun to establish a distinct screen image, and he began to borrow from past performances. His Nelson is therefore something of a summary of his matinee-idol roles, containing as it does suggestions of the obsessed, passionate characters of *Wuthering Heights* and *Rebecca*, the Fairbanks heroics of *Fire Over England*, and the propriety of Darcy. The character, though, is superficially conceived, and, as both public figure and man in love, Olivier's Nelson lacks real authority and passion. Olivier is reserved, his power held severely in check; his acting here lacks the quicksilver intensity and the romantic sweep of his earlier heroes.

That Hamilton Woman, unfortunately, is the only notable film costarring Olivier and Vivien Leigh. They are responsive to each other, but the slick popularization and the unbalanced roles prevent them from being seen at their best. Emma is a more fully developed and idiosyncratic character than Nelson, and Leigh is more animated than Olivier, playing the heroine as an English version of Scarlett O'Hara. Vivacious and sentimental, yet always genteel, Leigh looks like a full-fledged movie star while this time Olivier is content, gallantly, to be a subdued supporting player.

Throughout the 1940s and much of the 1950s, they were the most

celebrated theatrical couple in the world, socializing with the aristocracy, entertaining the famous at both their London townhouse
and at Notley Abbey, their country manor. Their activities provided
numerous items for both fan magazines and gossip columns. They
were a kind of international royalty, ornaments to café society,
courted, feted, and admired wherever they went.

And yet their marriage had enormous strains. Beautiful and
talented, Vivien Leigh was an acute manic-depressive whose wild
mood shifts were intensified by the pressures of her marriage to
Olivier. She regarded her husband as the greatest actor in the
world, and the thought that she would never be able to match his
level of achievement continuously gnawed at her. She was never
particularly impressed with her successes in films; that her performances in *Gone With the Wind* and *A Streetcar Named Desire* (1951)
are two of the greatest in film history was of less importance to her
than her desire to prove herself as a classical actress. By choice, she
made very few films, in order to concentrate on theater; but her
light voice and her personality didn't register as well on stage as on
film—her delivery of Shakespearean dialogue usually conveyed a
sense of strain, of hard work. The Oliviers made no films together
after *That Hamilton Woman*, but they acted together on stage frequently, in London for the Old Vic and on worldwide tours in a
number of classic plays including *Macbeth, Titus Andronicus,
Coriolanus, The School for Scandal*, and *Antony and Cleopatra*.
Among modern plays, they starred in Terence Rattigan's *The
Sleeping Prince*, Thornton Wilder's *The Skin of Our Teeth*, and
Shaw's *Caesar and Cleopatra*.

Leigh's insecurity was aggravated by critics who accused her of
diminishing Olivier's power. Kenneth Tynan was the most vocal of
the critics who complained that Olivier gallantly acted down to
accommodate his wife, and Tynan's most stinging review of their
work together was of their *Cleopatra* productions in 1951: "There is
in Miss Leigh's Cleopatra [in *Antony and Cleopatra*] an arresting
streak of Jane Austen. She picks at the part with the daintiness of a
debutante called upon to dismember a stag, and her manners are
first-rate. . . . Miss Leigh's limitations have wider repercussions
than those of most actresses. Sir Laurence, with that curious
chivalry which some time or other blights the progress of every
great actor, gives me the impression that he subdues his blow-lamp
ebullience to match her. Blunting his iron precision, levelling away

his towering authority, he meets her halfway. Antony climbs down; and Cleopatra pats him on the head. A cat, in fact, can do more than look at a king: she can hypnotise him."³

Leigh herself became convinced that she was curbing Olivier's genius, and she reacted by becoming increasingly hostile and depressed. Her behavior was marked by sudden outbursts of irrationality and violence; she would swear profusely, pick up strange men off the street, have fits of hysteria followed by periods of prolonged physical collapse. Olivier stood by helplessly as his wife retreated into more heightened forms of mania. Gallantly, he shielded her as much as possible from publicity, yet his own resources were being heavily overtaxed. In 1953, while she was filming *Elephant Walk* in Ceylon, Vivien Leigh had a complete breakdown; she was flown back to England, where she withdrew to Notley Abbey for many months of seclusion and recuperation. From that point on, the relationship began to disintegrate, until the couple was entirely estranged by the time, in 1958, when Olivier was rehearsing for *The Entertainer* at the Royal Court and Leigh, who had no part in the play, would interrupt with irrelevant and often abusive criticism. It was during this period that Olivier met Joan Plowright, and he realized that he had no choice but to divorce Vivien Leigh.⁴ Like everything else concerned with the public aspect of his relationship with this deeply troubled woman, the divorce was handled with great tact and diplomacy. One of the most celebrated romances of the century ended with a show of public decorum masking private suffering.

3

Henry V

WHEN HE RETURNED TO ENGLAND, late in 1941, Olivier interrupted his career in order to serve in the Fleet Air Arm. In anticipation of military duty, he had even taken aviation lessons while he was still in California. He wanted very much to participate in the war, but he was not a success as a pilot, and he spent most of his time in routine bureaucratic assignments.

He performed excerpts from Shakespeare on radio, and on one of these broadcasts he read the stirring, patriotic speeches from *Henry V*. An enterprising producer who was listening was struck with the idea of making a rousing film spectacle of the play. Fillipo del Guidice (like Alexander Korda, another foreigner who settled in England) approached Olivier with his proposal. The actor was skeptical about the project because at the time he did not feel that Shakespeare could be transferred effectively to film, and because he had never really been interested in the character of Henry. But del Guidice, once possessed of an idea, was as persevering as Korda, and he finally convinced Olivier that the making of *Henry V* would be a real service to the country: in order to direct the film, Olivier was released from his commitments to the Fleet Air Arm.

There was good reason why Olivier was reluctant to attempt a film adaptation of Shakespeare. At this point, the record of Shakespeare on film was not high in achievement. There had been only a handful of films, none of which had been either financial or critical successes, and none of which had quite discovered how to treat the plays in a new medium.

The few films—the Mary Pickford–Douglas Fairbanks *Taming of the Shrew* (1929), the all-star William Dieterle–Max Reinhardt *A Midsummer Night's Dream* (1935), the Leslie Howard–Norma Shearer *Romeo and Juliet* (1936), the Paul Czinner *As You Like*

Olivier as Henry V with Renee Asherson and Ivy St. Helier in the courtship scene modeled on illustrations in the Medieval Book of Hours of the Duc de Berry.

It—had all stumbled in one way or another. In each case, the filmmakers proved too light in their grasp of either theatrical or cinematic style. Pickford and Fairbanks, like George Cukor, who directed *Romeo and Juliet*, were film people with scant theatrical training and only superficial acquaintance with Shakespeare's stagecraft or poetry. Czinner and Reinhardt, on the other hand, were experienced men of the theater who had little practical sense of how to construct a film. To assist Reinhardt, Warner Brothers even hired William Dieterle, one of its contract directors. Reinhardt came to the film with a legendary reputation as a director of stage spectacles in which his trademarks were the choreography of crowds and a striking use of chiaroscuro. His handling of light and shadow, and of massive orchestrated movement, was to have a profound influence on the *mise-en-scène* of German Expressionist films of the 1920s. Reinhardt composed stunning stage pictures, but his particular kind of spectacle and visual extravagance worked best within the confines of the proscenium rather than in the more open frame of the film. Although the excitement and the sense of occasion generated by his fabled stage productions were not transferred to his film of Shakespeare's play, *A Midsummer Night's Dream* was nonetheless the most imaginative of the pre-Olivier adaptations. Reinhardt does manage to give the material a sense almost of Germanic doom; despite its smiling movie stars (Mickey Rooney, James Cagney, Anita Louise, Olivia de Havilland, Joe E. Brown) and its expensive Hollywood packaging, the film discovers some of the darkness and moodiness of Shakespeare's comedy: Victor Jory's grim presence as Oberon casts a particular shadow over the revelry. In places, the film presents a telling visual contrast between the world of the forest and that of the court; the world, that is, of the unconscious, of the id unleashed, on the one hand, and the rational, civilized, daytime milieu of the court on the other. Working in an alien medium, Reinhardt doesn't establish a fluent rhythm; the story and the characters often look uncomfortable within the movie frame, but unlike the other bland adaptations, this one does have the sense of a strong sensibility struggling to interpret and to mold the material. For all its aura of discomfort, this *Midsummer Night's Dream* has temperament and at least the beginnings of an attempt to reimagine a play in film terms.

Olivier had the advantage over his predecessors of coming to the problems of adaptation with firm grounding in both film and theater. From the actor's point of view, he felt in complete command of the material; what he lacked at this time was experience as a director.

The earlier Shakespearean films did not find a suitable way of mixing the reality of the film world (or at least the kind of reality that audiences expected to see in a film) with the elements of fantasy and romance that dominate the plays. These films don't discover a visual framework that suitably enhances the difficult and unfamiliar language. The settings in these pioneer efforts are too heavy, at once too real and too unimaginative, and therefore in conflict with the poetry: the earthbound worlds that the films establish are too literal as a canvas against which to sound the glorious cadences of Shakespearean verse. And the film stars chosen to speak it were in most cases ill-prepared for the job.

Olivier was mindful of the kind of imaginative failure of these adaptations, and as he began to plan his film of *Henry V*, he was determined not to repeat the mistakes—the missed opportunities—that marred the earlier works. Like the other directors, however, Olivier acknowledged that he was after all making a film intended for general audiences and that he would have to make cuts and transpositions in Shakespeare's text: he could not approach the play as Holy Writ if he were to have a popular success. Adaptation could not mean either slavish imitation or duplication of the original; he would have to approach the play with a freer hand, a more wide-ranging imaginative and interpretive flair, than his intimidated predecessors had been able to manage.

His first concern was to find a way of easing audiences, many of whom might never have seen or read any Shakespeare, into the language that was so much more dense and complex than the usual verisimilitude of movie dialogue. He would have to teach moviegoers how to listen to the rhythms of Shakespearean meter. He reached a solution almost by accident. Originally, he had thought of ending the film with a scene in the Globe Theatre, thereby frankly acknowledging the theatrical origins of the material in general as well as the circumstances of the Globe Theatre setting in particular. Olivier quickly realized that framing the entire film with the Globe Theatre setting would be a novel and appropriate way of accommodating the theatrical nature of the language. The film begins and ends, then, as though it were a film record of a production of the play at the Globe—this ideal framework proves true both to the artifice of theater and the reality of films, containing as it does both the immediacy and "presentness" of a performance in the theater and the detachment and comparative objectivity of a realistic historical recreation of that performance.

Olivier knew, however, that no matter how inventively he used his camera in the Globe Theatre setting, he could not hold the attention of movie audiences within such a confined space. And so, after having established the theatrical core of the material, he could "open" up the play and take the action outside the Globe framework. And here, in the fluid handling of place and time, Shakespeare had already done the work for him. In their rapid shifts of setting and their elliptical handling of time, Shakespeare's open-form plays, in direct violation of the classical unities, are constructed like screenplays. Unfettered by the confines of the stage at his Globe Theatre, Shakespeare's imagination roamed the world: every play has multiple settings, and a discontinuous use of time. Changes of scene often have the effect of cuts in film, with a scene shift indicating an indeterminate lapse of time, from minutes to years.

Shakespeare's "filmic" use of time and place was possible because of the essentially unlocalized stage picture that was part of Elizabethan theatrical convention. Settings in the plays were indicated through the language or with a minimum of props (a throne to suggest a palace, for instance); the emblematic props could be carried on- and offstage quickly, and the flow of the action would not be impeded. A film, of course, could not use the unlocalized space of the Elizabethan stage without alienating movie audiences; yet Olivier was aware of the ineffectiveness of the realistic, literal settings of the preceding adaptations. What he felt was needed was a kind of compromise between theatrical abstraction and stylization on the one hand and cinematic mimesis on the other. Working closely with his art director, Roger Furse, he devised a layered, intricate visual style, so that his film offers a truly daring blend of the artificial and the real. Olivier challenges the convention that the film world— the world within the frame—must necessarily be real: once his film leaves the meticulously reconstructed Globe Theatre set, the backgrounds are patently fake, childlike, *unreal*. Olivier wanted to recreate the lush colors, the foreshortened perspective, the naive and charming depiction of space found in illuminated medieval manuscripts; his idea was to give the film the rich, gloriously colored texture of a Book of Hours.

No film had ever quite looked like this before; no film, especially one intended for general audiences, had risked such glaring depar-

tures from the tradition of cinematic realism. Olivier decidedly was
not interested in playing it safe in the way that the earlier, flatfooted
adaptations had. He wanted to meet Shakespeare on his own terms
in a new and for the most part untried medium: his goal was nothing
less than to adapt Shakespeare's most spectacular and "cinematic"
play into a rousing, visually striking movie.

The opening speech of the Chorus in *Henry V* laments the fact
that the stage on which the play is to be performed cannot
adequately represent the chronicle history's many changes of scene
and its climactic Battle at Agincourt:

> O for a Muse of fire, that would ascend
> The brightest heaven of invention!
> A kingdom for a stage, princes to act,
> And monarchs to behold the swelling scene!
> Then should the warlike Harry, like himself,
> Assume the port of Mars; and at his heels,
> Leash'd in like hounds, should famine, sword, and fire,
> Crouch for employment. But pardon, gentles all,
> The flat unraised spirit that hath dar'd
> On this unworthy scaffold to bring forth
> So great an object: can this cockpit hold
> The vasty fields of France? or may we cram
> Within this wooden O the very casques
> That did affright the air at Agincourt?
> O pardon! since a crooked figure may
> Attest in little place a million;
> And let us, ciphers to this great accompt,
> On your imaginary forces work.
> Suppose within the girdle of these walls
> Are now confin'd two mighty monarchies,
> Whose high upreared and abutting fronts
> The perilous narrow ocean parts asunder:
> Piece out our imperfections with your thoughts:
> Into a thousand parts divide one man,
> And make imaginary puissance;
> Think, when we talk of horses, that you see them
> Printing their proud hoofs i' the receiving earth;
> For 'tis your thoughts that now must deck out kings,
> Carry them here and there; jumping o'er times,
> Turning the accomplishment of many years
> Into an hour-glass: for the which supply,
> Admit me Chorus to this history. . . .

The Prologue is thus an astounding anticipation of film! The Chorus, apologizing for Shakespeare for the limitations of the theater, implies the need for a narrative medium more capable of handling the story's many changes of scene and its moments of high action. Though there may be some irony in Shakespeare's displeasure with the incompleteness of language, the apology spoken by the Chorus indicates that the playwright felt the need of greater visual embellishment than his open stage could provide, and of a medium more plastic and flexible than the stage of the Wooden O.

The miniature reconstruction of Elizabethan London used for the introduction and conclusion to *Henry V*.

On film, Olivier was able to give the play the full-dress treatment that Shakespeare certainly seemed to feel that the material needed; but at the same time he wanted to acknowledge the difference between the means available to him and those Shakespeare had to depend on, and he begins therefore with a precise reconstruction of the Elizabethan stage. The film opens, as it were, in the Shakespearean manner. Olivier's direction of this filmed theater sequence, however, is not static, for his camera tracks and pans and cranes from top to bottom of the playhouse, presenting in realistic detail the atmosphere of the theatrical occasion in Shakespeare's time. (Throughout the film, Olivier's use of the camera is vigorous, thereby opposing the closed and static space of the theatrical settings with the openness and fluidity available to the filmmaker.)

In the richly textured Globe Theatre prologue, a bustling crowd, with its array of social classes from foppish gentleman to ruffled market girl, mills in the pit and gallery as backstage the actors apply their makeup, and young boys get dressed up as girls. Once the performance begins, the actors are detached from their roles, breaking character to communicate with the clamoring audience (although historians have objected to Olivier's presentation of the Elizabethan audience, for contemporary evidence suggests that Shakespeare's audiences would have been as well-behaved as audiences today, the film's hectoring crowd is colorful and seems appropriate in spirit if not in fact.) Once Olivier as King Henry enters, the audience settles down, and the actors begin to enter more fully into their roles. The fiction that Olivier initially establishes—that we are witnessing a stage performance of the play—serves as a cushion for the poetry: the theatrical framing softens the difference between theater and film while frankly acknowledging it.

Olivier retains the playhouse setting for the expository court scenes; when the play shifts to Southampton as Henry begins his assault on France, the film moves away from the theater. The sets for most of the scenes that take place outside the Globe are childlike, with their unnatural perspectives and their pretty pastel colors. The abstract designs create an enchanting fairy-tale atmosphere that remains the dominant visual motif until the night before the Battle of Agincourt, when the film's palette darkens and real earth and sky frame the actors. The battle itself, which is the visual and dramatic climax of the material, is spectacularly realistic. After this sequence, the film returns to the Book of Hours settings and then concludes, as it began, with the realistically detailed, onstage performance at the Globe.

Henry V, then, risks astonishing leaps in style from the documentarylike texture of the opening to the airy, fanciful ambiance of the scenes preceding and surrounding the battle, to the thoroughly realistic presentation of Agincourt itself. The mixture of convention and realism, of abstract stylization and physical reality, of theater and film, is audacious and yet the wild conjunction of visual styles enhances the play. As in his two following Shakespearean adaptations, Oliver wanted to make the material accessible to general audiences, and his brightly colored sets and playful blend of styles may seem like so many tricks to distract movie audiences from the unfamiliar language by giving them luscious pictures to look at. At first, in the scenes set outside the Globe, the extreme stylization is startling, and we seem to be placed in the position of observers of an exotic ritual. But gradually, as if by a magical process, the strong, decorative visual designs take us into rather than away from story and characters: we're beguiled into involvement. Sliding along a curve of escalating realism in sets and acting, the film moves smoothly from one mode to the next.

Taking his cue from Shakespeare, Olivier has conceived the material as a series of visual set pieces. He has turned the history play into the film that Shakespeare, amazingly, seemed to predict was the appropriate medium for the story of the king's victory in France. In his first film, Olivier treats the medium as though it were an enchanting new toy, and his direction, filled as it is with discovery and experimentation, is exuberant. From the beginning, as the camera pans a remarkably detailed miniature of Elizabethan London, Olivier establishes movement as an integral part of his technique; the swooping, craning camerawork establishes at once the film's celebratory spirit. Olivier uses a panning, roving camera to establish connections between scenes as well; so, for instance, after Agincourt, the camera scans an empty landscape until it settles on a charming, snow-covered village scene, the color and design of which is patterned directly on a Book of Hours illustration. The moving, exploring camera functions throughout as a way of solidifying connections in time and place; Olivier was concerned that Shakespeare's "cuts" were often in fact too abrupt, that audiences might be disoriented as the action moves from one setting to the next, from England to France, and he tried to smooth the transitions, to make them less elliptical, through specifically cinematic means of linking different locations and periods of time.

His use of dissolves, pans, tracking shots—of different kinds of filmic transitions—is emphatic: *Henry V* does not disguise its syntax. Olivier reserves the most dazzling use of film punctuation, however, for the battle sequence. He studied the battle-on-the-ice episode in Eisenstein's *Alexander Nevsky* (1938), and his symmetrical arrangement of archers, his long shots of soldiers silhouetted against the horizon, and his dynamic cutting, acknowledge his debt to Eisenstein's epic. He creates tension by editing on conflicting directions of movement: a shot of horses charging from left to right of the frame is balanced, in the following shot, by a countermovement from right to left. Cuts are matched to the swelling cadences of William Walton's pageantlike score, which parallels Prokofieff's for *Alexander Nevsky* in its enhancement of the images. The most exciting moment in the film is the long tracking shot of the charge of the French soldiers. Olivier had a railroad track built on which he mounted his camera, and the effect of the camera moving forward at the same lunging pace as the horses is thrilling (though, politically, it would have been more appropriate if English rather than French warriors had supplied this moment of military glory). Olivier said at the time that he was not, after all, a big battle director and that he did not want to compete with Cecil B. De Mille; but the Agincourt sequence in *Henry V*, filmed in Ireland over a thirty-nine-day period and lasting on screen for ten minutes, is one of the most skillfully choreographed military clashes in film. Photographed beneath a sharp blue sky on a vast plain surrounded by lush greenery, the grand battle is crucial in establishing the film's patriotic spirit.

The Agincourt scenes are hectically edited to create a surging, thrusting momentum; the camerawork is athletic. For the scenes in the French court, however, Olivier uses a very different kind of syntax; here, his camera and style of editing are notably sedate. Enclosed by pillars and arches, the French noblemen occupy separate "frames." The composition is deliberately stiff; and the ornamental scenes among the squabbling, dimwitted French lack the fluency of the corresponding scenes of Henry and his men. The film is less sympathetic than Shakespeare to the French; their court is designed in a fragile and almost childlike manner, and the king and his advisers are played, for the most part, as buffoons.

Like *Fire Over England* and *That Hamilton Woman, Henry V* was made to bolster English morale during a period of national crisis, and so Henry is presented as an idealized leader of his country, courageous in battle, benevolent, firm, wise. The film erases most of the darker tones of Shakespeare's denser and more complex psychological portrait of Henry; Olivier's king is a less intricate, and much less ambivalent, character than Shakespeare's original.

Almost all the cuts and changes in the text are dictated by the need to make a rousing patriotic spectacle. In order to present the British as a staunchly unified force, Olivier and his associates Alan Dent and Dallas Bower eliminate the characters of Cambridge, Scroop, and Grey, who collaborate with the French and whom Henry sentences to death. Henry's threats before Harfleur, with their images of sexual violation, are omitted, as are his equally fierce warnings to the French King Charles and his injunction to his soldiers to cut the throats of their prisoners. Olivier omits Henry's concern, on the eve before Agincourt, of inheriting his father's guilt (Henry IV usurped the crown from Richard II).

At the beginning of the film, Olivier deliberately deflates the scene in which churchmen urge the king to make war. Their arguments for England's claims to France are self-serving and historically ill-founded. In the play, this early scene, following the Chorus's rousing prologue, establishes an atmosphere of political double-dealing and of a suspect alliance between Church and State. Olivier directs the scene as farce; the clergymen are fools who get entangled in scrolls and masses of paper as they attempt, ineptly, to offer their justifications for war. Olivier does not want the audience to concentrate on the ambiguous political motivations of the English, and he shapes the material in such a way that Henry is provoked into war against the French when the arrogant French ambassador taunts him with a presentation of tennis balls, thereby mocking him for his former way of life when he cavorted irresponsibly in the company of Falstaff.

Cuts, then, are made to simplify and to sweeten the political context. The tyrannical outbursts, the threats of violence, that complicate and shadow Shakespeare's treatment of Henry are resolutely erased. Much more than the play, the film stresses the difference between the proud, assertive, disciplined English and the bickering, simpering French. But *Henry V* is not the mindlessly patriotic display of jingoism that it is often accused of being: Olivier does try for some balance and shading in the film's attitude toward war. After

Agincourt, the camera roams the deserted battlefield, strewn with the bodies of both English and French soldiers, as a single riderless horse, a powerful if conventional emblem of death, wanders among the dead. On the soundtrack, a "Te Deum" underscores the melancholy imagery. The heroic moments in the film are reserved for the English, but Olivier extends to the defeated French a scene that allows them some nobility: as the Duke of Burgundy laments his country's fate, the camera peers outside the arched windows of the French court to reveal a gray, denuded landscape. The parched countryside is eloquent testimony to the costs of war.

If, under the pressures of contemporary history, Olivier's interpretation is idealized and romantic, he has nonetheless introduced a few dark notes, apparent also in his handling of the comic characters. His treatment of Falstaff is especially somber. He interpolates Falstaff's death scene (from *2 Henry IV*, 5:5) in which the old braggart soldier recalls his rejection by the new king. Falstaff is presented, curiously, not as the overstuffed, Rabelaisian figure of comic tradition, but as a frail, almost ghostlike figure—a mask of death. George Robey, a music-hall comic who plays the role, speaks his few lines in a faltering whisper. This striking image of man's mortality is placed between Henry's rousing speech to his men at Southampton and the first scene set in the weak and preoccupied French court. Falstaff's death, performed in the semirealistic Boar's Head setting, in muted lighting, thus acts as a transition between the nationalist energy of the English and the enervation of the French court. The autumnal interlude is no doubt intended to underscore Henry's rejection of his younger self, his frivolous days as a roustabout: now that Henry is king, and military leader, he must banish Falstaffism. But the ambiguous scene, coming where it does, after Henry's stirring speech to his men, acts as a kind of corrective to the image of Henry's vitality: Falstaff's deathbed scene serves as a reminder of the mortality and frailty of all men.

The comic characters are used throughout to demonstrate the effects of war on the "common" folk. Olivier trims the play's abundant low comic subplot to a bare minimum, employing the trio of Bardolph, Nym, and Pistol as a sometimes-mocking and sometimes-melancholy chorus to the public themes of heroism and military victory. One of the film's most moving moments is Pistol's revelation to Fluellen, after he has been humiliated by him, that his wife, Nell, has died.

When the comic characters do not comment on the war, when they simply chide and taunt each other in scenes of rustic humor, the film is remarkably flat. In these passages, as nowhere else, the direction is stagy. The camera remains stationary as the characters challenge each other: the actors are stranded in a neutral space that is neither clearly theatrical nor cinematic as they harangue each other in densely idiomatic language that is virtually impenetrable. These low-comedy contretemps are an interference since Olivier hasn't connected them meaningfully to the historical pageantry that is his principal concern. Filmed in a perfunctory, almost absentminded manner, the halting, static, unintelligible scenes of comic interplay among the gruff comedians never achieve a rhythm of their own and, more crucially, they have no sense of fun.

Olivier's own performance is of course influenced by the simplified political framework and the general pattern of chastening and softening to which the play has been submitted. Drawn to characters with a more complex and gnarled psychology than Henry's, Olivier was never fully engaged by Shakespeare's warrior king, even when he had played Shakespeare's full, and more multi-colored, character on stage at the Old Vic in 1937. Given the circumstances under which the film was made, he was necessarily restricted to a straightforward and idealistic reading of the role. Valorous, humane, unfaltering, with only dim traces of the Falstaffism of his younger days, Olivier's king is a glorious leader. At a different time, he might have amplified the fact that Henry is something of an actor who works himself up into giving frenzied pep talks to his soldiers: there is something artificial and studied about this conscientious ruler (characteristics that are suggested in *Henry IV, Parts I* and *II*), but Olivier only lightly sketches in the king's poseur qualities. Appropriately, though, in the opening scenes in the playhouse, he plays like a renowned actor, in a deliberately orotund style. We see him first offstage, coughing as he prepares for his entrance, and then later, after his scene, shaking hands with the actor who played the Archbishop of Canterbury. On the Globe stage, Olivier's diction is overly precise, his pacing deliberate, his tone stentorian. He is edging his way into the character, and the sense of performance slyly underscores an important point about this most image-conscious of monarchs. Though the theatricality remains a part of his interpretation, it is toned down once the film leaves the Wooden O.

Like Titus Andronicus and Coriolanus, two other roles in which

Olivier was particularly successful, Henry is a character who plays to
the crowd and who is always on public display. Olivier's extroverted, ringing delivery emphasizes the character's statesmanlike
grandeur. His king is a skillful orator, an accomplished man of affairs, a calculating public personality; but Olivier is careful to make
him likable rather than obviously devious like Richard III.

Olivier shrewdly uses the camera to heighten his performance by
reversing the usual method of filming monologues. Olivier had
noticed, in the earlier adaptations, that the directors would inevitably film a lengthy speech by beginning with a long shot and moving
gradually to a close-up. Since the emotional rhythm of the speeches
is usually in precisely the opposite direction, the camera undercut
the actor's momentum: the close-up at the end of the monologue or
soliloquy forced the actor to modulate his delivery at just the point
he should be most impassioned. Instead of moving the camera in as
the king's set speeches reach their climax, thereby forcing him to
subdue his intensity, he begins with a close-up and then has the
camera pull back to a high-angle overhead shot as Henry's excitement builds, thereby freeing him to pitch his delivery to the top-
row balcony. For both the play's famous monologues, in which
Henry inspires his men to military glory—"Once more unto the
breach" (3:1) and the St. Crispin's Day oration that precedes the
Battle of Agincourt (4:3)—Olivier, in tight close-up, begins quietly,
as if he is speaking only to the soldiers nearest him. As he works
himself up to a rhetorical frenzy, the craning camera retreats to a
striking high-angle long shot, and he is free to explode, the climax of
the speeches delivered in a ringing, thunderous bellow that is exhilarating.

In the scenes before Agincourt, Shakespeare interrupts the historical pageantry that is the play's dominant mode by showing us
private glimpses of the king. Fittingly, Olivier plays these moments
in an entirely different register from the rest of his performance. As
he moves through the camp, talking (in disguise, pretending to be a
common soldier) to his men, musing on the demands of ceremony,
he is pleasingly mellow; we get fleeting impressions of the private
man who exists beneath the king's robes. The stark chiaroscuro of
these scenes, which makes them visually distinct from the rest of the
film, enforces the sense that we are seeing a new facet of the character.

Olivier provides further tonal variation in the final courtship scenes with the French princess. Here, in contrast to the stentorian quality of Henry's public moments, he performs with a beguiling lightness. He is again role-playing, slyly presenting himself as a rough warrior lacking in courtly graces; but the actor makes light of the king's evident manipulation, and the wooing scene provides a charming grace note to the performance and the film.

Within a modest range, then, Olivier discovers some variety in this least dramatically challenging of Shakespeare's monarchs; his performance has shadows amid the highlights. Olivier finds warmth and humor in a role that is conceived primarily as a series of set speeches and calculated public moments: it would indeed be possible to play Henry as a crafty warmonger, a Machiavellian orchestrator of political opinion.

Olivier's performance dominates the film, as of course it must, but as director and fellow actor, he has allowed his supporting cast moments of their own. In this film, as in his two later adaptations, Olivier has obtained performances of uniform excellence from his company. Unlike the earlier Shakespearean films, the actors here treat the verse as verse, directly, forthrightly, without apology or compromise. Olivier's cast, all experienced classical actors, revel in the cadences, the rolling periods and thunderous climaxes, of Shakespeare's vigorous poetry. This was the first time on film that Shakespeare was performed with such confidence and élan; there is no condescension to a new medium, or to the popular audiences for whom the film was intended. The verse is read quickly, crisply, with no sacrifice of rhythm or meter, without patronizing regard as to whether or not movie audiences will be able to "get" every word. The rhetorical flourish of the acting is established at once in Lesley Banks's spirited reading of the Chorus. Framed by the Globe Theatre setting, the cunning play-within-a-play format, Banks is free to deliver his lines with unhesitating theatrical gusto. His manner is hardy and energetic: we're hearing the full melody of Shakespeare's verse.

Olivier and Banks, both in a sense acting as masters of ceremonies, perform in a more robust style than the other actors. The characters not enclosed by the theatrical frame—the comic characters, the French King Charles, the Princess Katharine, the Duke of Burgundy—are necessarily seen in smaller scale. Robert Newton as Pistol and Freda Jackson as Mistress Quickly are especially effective in revealing the melancholy quality of the comic figures; they play with a quiet pathos that provides a needed counterpoint to Olivier's stirring public moments. As the coy, virginal French princess and her wry handmaiden, Renee Asherson and Ivy St. Helier are delectable. The droll scene in which the princess is given her English lesson, replete with glancing double entendres, is irresistible; the charm and delicacy of the actresses are matched by the fanciful pink garden in which their exchange is set.

Harcourt Williams's querulous, desiccated French king, frail of voice and body, also has a wonderfully dry comic quality and hints of pathos. Olivier allows the French a delicate irony that provides a contrast to the bellicose Englishmen and that enriches the film's tone. Perhaps the subtlest performance among the French characters is Jonathan Field's as Montjoy, the French Herald. Each time he has an interview with Henry, he changes his tone; from the mocking, insolent attitude he uses in the first encounter, to the respect he shows in the last meeting, his shifting responses mirror audience reaction; with him, we share a sense of the king's skill and fortitude, his heroic determination.

From a play that glorifies war and military conquest and from a screenplay that erases many of the knots that Shakespeare introduced to darken material that did not fully engage him, Olivier has created a stirring epic that mixes personal drama with the dominant pageantry. Both for his truly innovative direction and his own commanding performance, *Henry V* is one of the triumphs of his career.

When it was released in 1945, the film was greeted with much, though not universal, enthusiasm. Most contemporary critics hailed it for its stylistic daring, its respect for Shakespeare's language, and its historical importance as the first fully realized Shakespearean adaptation on film. Those who disliked the film generally did so for its handling of the comic characters, for its mixture of visual styles, or for its propagandistic elements. The most negative reaction among serious critics was Manny Farber's. Farber, a writer who much prefers the gritty, action-filled B movie to the high art of Shakespeare, attacked the film's design: "*Henry V* always looks a bit contrived (stagy and toylike), boyish, and heavy with decor and costuming the way a grade-school operetta is." Elliott Norton and Philip Hartung complained of the jingoistic interpretation: "The voice is the voice of Shakespeare, but the hand is sometimes the hand of Brendan Bracken, who was England's minister of information when the picture was made." "Anti-Britishers may have some

cause to complain that the English are again praising themselves
and shooting their tops off about their own wares."[1]

Among the chorus of praise and acclamation, James Agee's famous, loving, two-part appreciation in the *Nation* was the sweetest
and the wisest. Although Agee applauded the film primarily for its
respect for Shakespeare's language rather than for its film sense or
its original use of the medium, his piece nonetheless remains the
final word on Olivier's landmark achievement: "[The] branching,
nervous interpretive intelligence, so contemporary in quality except
that it always keeps the main lines of its drive and meaning clear,
never spiraling or strangling in awareness, is vivid in every way
during all parts of the film. . . . Mr. Olivier and his associates . . .
have done somewhere near all that talent, cultivation, taste, knowl-
edgeability, love of one's work—every excellence, in fact, short of
genius—can be expected to do; and that, the picture testifies, is a
very great deal. . . . I am not a Tory, a monarchist, a Catholic, a
medievalist, an Englishman, or, despite all the good that it engen-
ders, a lover of war: but the beauty and power of this traditional
exercise was such that, watching it, I wished I was, thought I was,
and was proud of it."[2]

Henry V was a financial success as well, enjoying long first-run
engagements in major cities. In New York, it played for a year at the
City Center, the first and only time in its history that this cavernous
house (normally reserved for dance) was used for screening a film.
Olivier's film helped to revive the fortunes of the post-war British
film industry as much as Korda's production of *The Private Life of
Henry VIII* had stimulated it a decade earlier. In the 1940s, still
suffering under the quota law, whereby a certain number of British
films had to be made in order for distributors to import the more
commercially desirable Hollywood movies, British films nonetheless began to achieve a national sensibility in ways that the more
international flavor of the Korda productions of the 1930s had not.
Britain's devastating experience in World War II gave filmmakers a
subject to deal with, and modest contemporary films like David
Lean's *Brief Encounter* and Noel Coward's *In Which We Serve*
reflected social and political reality. The postwar renaissance of the
British film, then, in which distinctly British themes and settings
were presented in ways that interested worldwide audiences, was in
good measure inaugurated by Olivier's rousing, patriotic *Henry V*, a
paean to national glory.

4

Hamlet

HENRY V established Olivier as a great film actor. At the time, however, he had not yet established himself onstage as a preeminent classical performer. His seasons at the Old Vic under Tyrone Guthrie's management in 1937 and 1938 were certainly evidence of a formidable talent, but Olivier's genius was inchoate rather than fully matured. He came into his own as an interpreter of Shakespeare only after his appearance on film as Henry, in the now-legendary seasons at the Old Vic from 1944 to 1946.

Following the war (and no doubt influenced by his achievement with *Henry V*), Olivier was asked, along with Ralph Richardson and John Burrell, to assume management of the Old Vic. This was his first venture into theatrical management; later, he was to go into production at the St. James Theatre, and he was director of the Chichester Theatre Festival in 1961 and of the National Theatre from 1963 to 1973. In recognition of his work at the Old Vic, Olivier was knighted in the Birthday Honors List in January, 1947.

It was during this most creative phase of his career that Olivier, prodded once again by Fillipe del Guidice, undertook his second Shakespearean adaptation. In making *Hamlet* (in 1947), Olivier was concerned, as he had been with *Henry V*, about avoiding the static quality of filmed theater. Without sacrificing the integrity of the play, he wanted to give visual fluency to theatrical material. *Hamlet*, of course, is radically different from *Henry V*, and in moving from the extroverted spectacle of the chronicle play to Shakespeare's most introverted chamber drama, Olivier altered his style severely: the dark, moody, claustrophobic atmosphere of this second adaptation provides a striking contrast to the bright holiday tones of *Henry*.

Unlike the historical pageant, *Hamlet* takes place within a single

79

Olivier as Hamlet.

basic setting, the Castle at Elsinore, and so there are fewer opportunities for visual expansion of the text. Unlike the innovative designs for the earlier film, Olivier's concept here, devised in close
consultation with Roger Furse, is one that is standard for the play.
Furse has written that their design for the castle is deliberately
traditional, that it respects "preconceptions about *Hamlet*," and that
it is intended therefore to underscore the fact that the hero is "the
eternal and universal 'man who cannot make up his mind.' . . . It
was undesirable that the castle should be constructed in such a way
as to recall too insistently any particular point in time or space. We
wanted neither a copy of the real castle in Denmark nor the formal
background of Shakespeare's theatre which you saw in *Henry V*."[1]
Set in cavernous, sparsely furnished rooms in which the vast space is
fragmented by arches, stairways, platforms, and columns, the film
creates a deliberately closed environment. The dark, mostly bare
rooms, and the vast, empty spaces are meant to be projections of
Hamlet's tormented consciousness. In a muted way, therefore, the
film's method is expressionist, its dark exterior world correlating to
Hamlet's inner doubts, uncertainties, irresolutions. Strong contrasts
between light and shadow also underscore the expressionist atmosphere as characters are sometimes picked out from the swelling,
enveloping darkness by a theatrical spotlight. As Roger Furse has
written, "The actors and the lighting are the only means of composition within the setting." One of the most effective examples of the
essentially theatrical and expressionistic chiaroscuro lighting occurs
when the players, summoned by Hamlet, make their first entrance
amid a blaze of torches: the burst of light that accompanies their
appearance provides a startling counterpoint to the dark, isolated
image of Hamlet that precedes their scene. They seem to have
materialized out of the depths of Hamlet's subconscious, brought to
the surface to assist the Prince in his scheme to entrap Claudius.

    Hamlet, then, avoids the dazzling colors and the surprising decor
of *Henry V*. The cold, bare, gloomy castle, though, and the stark
black-and-white photography, with its sharp contrasts between light
and shadow, have a strong visual impact. More conventional in its
design than the earlier film, *Hamlet* still makes a bold visual impression. In terms of its decor and its chiaroscuro, the film is blatantly
theatrical, but, as in *Henry*, Olivier's use of space is wonderfully
fluid, open-ended. His camera work, even more than in the earlier
film, is aggressively mobile. The movement of the camera enlarges

the frame in which the drama is enacted, converting the closed space of the theater into filmic openness and endlessness. The inquisitive, roving camera, craning up and down stairways, peering into private bedchambers, lunging down labyrinthine castle corridors to eavesdrop on whispered exchanges or lovers' quarrels or royal scandals, becomes a character in its own right, an extension of the audience's curiosity. Despite the expressionist tendency of the decor, the point of reference remains, for the most part, outside Hamlet: this is not a tricky, subjective rendering of the story, as if told from within Hamlet's consciousness. The point of view shifts; at brief moments, we see the action as Hamlet or Ophelia or the Ghost sees it, but primarily the camera presents an outside view of the drama, that of an observer searching the castle for clues and explanations.

The almost constantly traveling camera provides continuity of place and action, thereby erasing the sharp divisions between act and scene that are part of Shakespeare's narrative construction. Olivier preserves spatial and temporal integrity by combining the moving camera with long takes. Transitions, typically, are made by moving the camera through hallways and up and down stairs rather than by conventional cutting. Sometimes, as the camera dollies down a corridor, carrying us to the next scene, there is a series of dissolves which seem to move us further into the action, as if we are penetrating a maze.

In his handling of time and place, then, Olivier stresses continuity rather than separation. The film has a self-consciously fluent and graceful movement, a sense of wholeness rather than fragmentation: individual scenes have a minimum of editing, and scenes are combined into sequences by the roving camera rather than by cuts. As a result, the film has a liquid, flowing quality which contributes substantially to the dreamlike ambiance, the lyrical haze in which the action seems to be suspended.

By now an avid student of the cinema, Olivier this time studied Orson Welles rather than Eisenstein, using the deep focus and long takes associated with Wellesian *mise-en-scène* as opposed to the Eisensteinian montage he employed for depicting the Battle of Agincourt in *Henry V*. *Mise-en-scène* in *Hamlet*, in fact, becomes an integral expression of theme. Within the same shot, characters are often separated from each other by vast spaces; the use of deep focus allows us to see characters in the rear of the frame, at the end of long corridors or across large rooms, and the physical separation, realistically rendered, is emblematic of the emotional distance or the distrust between characters. The kind of separation between characters, made possible through deep focus, serves throughout as a visual signal of Hamlet's estrangement from everyone else. There is an especially inventive use of deep focus early in the film as Hamlet, on the ramparts, oversees the revelry of the court in the castle below. Seeing Hamlet and the revelers at Claudius's party in the same shot offers a powerful image of Hamlet's isolation from the social world of the court.

This method of separation within the frame is particularly forceful in dramatizing the growing alienation between Hamlet and Ophelia. The image of a shrunken Ophelia, framed by pillars in the rear of the screen as Hamlet, in the foreground, rants at her, boldly underlines their ruptured relationship.

Olivier's shrewd placement of his actors within the frame is frequently emblematic. A good example is the comic passage in which Hamlet mercilessly mocks Polonius. Book in hand, Hamlet walks on a raised platform while the fawning Polonius, standing on the floor below, looks up at him. This positioning of the actors nicely underscores Hamlet's play-acting: he is literally on a stage, "playing" to the gullible Polonius beneath him. Hamlet's raised position emphasizes his self-appointed role as mocking lord of the revels, as skillful actor weaving webs in which to ensnare not only the foolish, prating Polonius but the cunning Claudius as well.

Olivier's methods, like those of Orson Welles, are both realistic (deep focus, the long take) and expressionistic (chiaroscuro, setting as emanations of character). At times, Olivier uses devices that are meant to extend the sense of reality in which the action takes place; at other points, his approach is intentionally stylized and abstract.

One of his techniques for giving the play realistic touches are the glimpses of the "real" world beyond the castle. In several scenes, in the depth of the frame, there are views of hills and trees that look like the natural world as it appears in the backgrounds of Renaissance portraits. As further "evidence" of reality, Olivier begins and ends the film with a shot of rolling waves. In the graveyard scene, there is real earth. Gertrude's account of Ophelia's death is accompanied by an image of Ophelia floating in a stream (the composition is based on the Millais painting in the Tate Gallery). As Horatio reads Hamlet's letter, we see the pirates' attack on Hamlet's ship.

Olivier anticipated that these efforts to open up the play, to introduce elements of the world beyond Elsinore Castle, would displease some audiences: "It will, I dare say, be objected that the sea-fight should not have been included. . . . But as I see it, it is not to be imagined that the Shakespeare who wrote parts for opposing armies, and tried to turn his little riverside stage into the scenes of Antony's fall and Prospero's island, would not have eagerly welcomed the means to show these places more realistically, if they had been to his hand. Nothing that we know of Shakespeare suggests that he actually enjoyed being 'cabin'd, cribb'd, confined' by the rudimentary conditions of the stage for which he wrote."[2]

These scattered attempts to open up the film to the real world outside are not well handled technically. The idea of providing a visual counterpoint to the interior world of Elsinore is valid, but the reality that Olivier presents looks fake: the ships in the sea battle are clearly miniatures; the image of Ophelia floating in a real stream looks posed; in the rear of the shot of breaking waves there is a view of the fog-enshrouded castle that is patently phony. Paradoxically, when the film remains within the realistically rendered space of the castle, it looks "real"; when it ventures, briefly and ineffectively, out into what is supposed to be the world of nature, it looks artificial.

Olivier's attempts to enclose the action by references to nature are more successfully managed in his use of the sound of breaking waves as aural punctuation throughout the scenes on the ramparts. Here, without disruption or strain, the inclusion of an aspect of the real world expands the sense of space in which the drama is played, opens it up to reality.

Typical of his methods, though, Olivier mixes natural sound in the scenes on the ramparts with the expressionistic sound of an ominous echoing heartbeat that is used whenever the Ghost appears. This distorted and symbolic sound (which represents "the excited pulse of any of the people who become conscious of the presence of the Ghost," writes Alan Dent in the published screenplay for the film) is reminiscent of the echo-chamber effects in *Citizen Kane*.

Like his soundtrack, Olivier's camera work also includes both realistic and expressionistic techniques. If the camera is often used to create a sense of real space, it serves sometimes for exactly the opposite effect. The action is punctuated with virtuoso high-angle shots that, like Welles's celebrated low angles, distort our percep-

Hamlet goes to meet the ghost of his father on the turrets of Elsinor Castle.

tions of physical reality. At the beginning of the film, there is an extreme high-angle shot of the night watch, spotlighted on the ramparts and surrounded by fog and eerie darkness. The exaggerated composition aggressively shatters the closed space of the theatrical proscenium and announces Olivier's intentions of transforming a play into a film.

Hamlet's fogbound encounter with the Ghost—the most expressionistic scene in the film—is rendered with startling shifts in point of view. When Hamlet first sees the Ghost, the image zooms in and out of focus in imitation of the magnified heartbeats on the soundtrack. At the end of the confrontation, as Hamlet collapses amid swirling fog, the camera cranes up to another vertiginous angle.

The film has many visual set pieces. Sometimes the vignettes or cameos are used to offset what Olivier feared might be the static quality of longer set speeches and soliloquies. When Ophelia tells her father and the king about Hamlet's entry into her closet, the encounter, beginning and ending with an iris shot, is reenacted in mime. We see the death of Hamlet's father in his garden as the Ghost describes it to the distraught prince. Olivier retains only two soliloquies—"To be or not to be" (3:1) and "O that this too too solid flesh" (1:2). Both are performed with a disorienting blend of voiceover and direct address. The voiceover technique is a strained way of suggesting thought: the separation of voice and image creates distance between the audience and the actor, and makes the soliloquies seem unnecessarily remote. "To be or not to be" is especially mishandled. Olivier sets it on the ramparts, with Hamlet posed in profile against a fake studio sky. The natural sound of the waves mixes with William Walton's heavy-handed score, used all too obviously to "point" the speech. The combination, in both sound and image, of reality and artifice, of cinematic intimacy and theatrical convention, is jarring, and the uneasy mingling of styles is enhanced rather than resolved by the intrusive shot of the breaking waves, as Hamlet tosses his dagger into the ocean, that serves as a visual period to the soliloquy.

Roger Furse has defended the choice of "the dizzy height" of the topmost tower of the battlements as setting for the soliloquy by suggesting that the speech is "a meditation on suicide" and "the means of suicide are very close at hand." The placement of the soliloquy looks less like a means of thematic enhancement, however, than a half-hearted way of opening up the drama by giving it variety of setting and texture.

The showy direction in the public scenes—the royal processions, the court fanfare— is more successful than the attempts to embellish some of the intimate moments. The play-within-the-play and the final duel, in particular, have real bravado. In the play scene, the camera moves in semicircular rotation as it peers onto the players from behind the heads of the royal audience. As the actors perform in mime (the dumb show replaces the spoken *Murder of Gonzago* used in the play), the repetitive camera movement becomes an essential means of heightening tension and, as Jack J. Jorgens notes, "is a symbol of the impossibility of fixity in a world of flux."[3] The tracking camera, presenting the play as Hamlet, Ophelia, Claudius, Gertrude, and Polonius see it, underlines the shifting point of view that has been a recurrent device throughout the film. The lighting from below in this scene casts sinister shadows on faces, and the low angle on Claudius as he shouts "Give me light!" is especially effective. The scene concludes with a series of quick cuts that underscore the chaos that the king's outburst has created.

In the theater, the final duel between Hamlet and Laertes often seems anticlimactic. Olivier, however, gives full value to the scene. The court ceremony that surrounds and comments on the duel is vigorously directed, with the actors responding like a well-drilled ensemble to the brisk sword play. Through a more fragmented editing style than that used elsewhere in the film, Olivier builds an atmosphere of mounting excitement that is capped by Hamlet's daring leap onto Claudius from a high balcony.

Olivier matches the duel scene with his concluding tour de force: as Hamlet's body is borne to the height of the turrets for royal burial, the camera follows the pallbearers up the winding stairs in an unbroken crane shot, and as the mourners ascend, flashes of lightning illuminate the various rooms—Claudius's closet, Gertrude's bedroom, the throne room—in which key points of the drama have been enacted. This visual coda acts as both summary and apotheosis; ending in long shot with figures silhouetted against a lowering sky, the final procession is a kind of Stations of the Cross that elevates Hamlet to mythic dimensions.

This last virtuoso camera work repeats (in reverse) the film's opening movement—these descending and ascending tracking shots thus enclose the film in an imposing framework. "I doubt whether it [carrying Hamlet's body to the topmost tower] could be defended logically," notes Roger Furse. "But logic and dramatic fitness are not the same thing. Thousands of years ago it was the custom to bury warriors on high places of the hills. Towers have often symbolized in literature the dwellings of meditative, self-questioning men. For such reasons, more sympathetic to the imagination than to logic, it is appropriate that Hamlet's body should be taken there."[4] The grand procession to the top of the castle that closes the film implies a healing and resurrection that some critics have objected to as being false to Shakespeare's more muted ending. The film "concludes with a crescendo of regeneration," Jack Jorges writes. "Shakespeare's sense of waste and ambivalent blend of triumph and defeat give way to an unequivocal sense of fulfillment."[5]

Making their *Hamlet* for a wider audience than would ever see it on the stage, Olivier and Alan Dent had to decide on many cuts. "I could only make what I called at the time a study in *Hamlet*," Olivier has said. "I had to make it acceptable, without making it vulgarly popular; tasteful, but entertaining, which Shakespeare at his best is."[6] In choosing what to cut, Olivier and Dent were guided by four basic considerations: reducing the length (performing the full version, which is rarely done even in the theater, would take well over four hours), clarifying the plot, removing obscure language, and making the material as accessible as possible to general audiences, who may have had little or no experience with Shakespeare. Olivier was mindful as well of the fact that "the cinema is even more insistent on the visual aspect of art than the theatre, that the camera can, and must, nose into corners and magnify details that escape notice or pass muster on the stage. On the screen, too, the essential consideration is for what is seen, and characters or passages of poetry that may be kept in the theatre, on account of their intrinsic interest or beauty respectively, cannot be reconciled with the more closely-knit demands of a two-hour film."[7]

With these considerations of length and clarity in mind, Olivier and Dent excised the minor characters of Voltimand, Cornelius, Reynaldo, and the Second Gravedigger, and the more significant figures of Fortinbras, and Rosencrantz and Guildenstern as well. Alan Dent explains the elimination of Rosencrantz and Guildenstern on the grounds that "there just had to be one whacking great cut at the very outset—one preliminary tremendous sacrifice, if the film were not to run to the impracticable length of three hours or more."[8] They reduced the number of soliloquies and cut passages from many of the longer speeches; and they rearranged the order of some of the scenes. Their decision, from the beginning, was to sacrifice the political and social context of the war between Denmark and Norway that provides an image of the public world in favor of concentrating on the purely private drama of Hamlet's inner conflicts.

Two great soliloquies—"O what a rogue and peasant slave" (2:2) and "How all occasions do inform against me" (4:4)—are cut because the adapters felt that the eloquence of these passages, while enlarging the psychological and philosophical dimension of the drama, materially slowed down the action. "To be or not to be" is placed to follow Hamlet's brutal treatment of Ophelia in the nunnery scene rather than after Hamlet's decision to trap Claudius with *The Murder of Gonzago*, where it appears in the play. Ophelia's madness, death, and funeral follow one upon the other in much faster sequence than in Shakespeare's original.

One of Olivier's most controversial decisions was to preface the film with a a speech from the play that suggests that Hamlet's problems are attributable to one flaw:

> So, oft if chances in particular men,
> That for some vicious mole of nature in them,
> By the o'er growth of some complexion,
> Oft breaking down the pales and forts of reason,
> Or by some habit that too much o'er-leavens
> The form of plausive manners, that these men,
> Carrying, I say, the stamp of one defect,
> Their virtues else, be they as pure as grace,
> Shall in the general censure take corruption
> From that particular fault.

The words appear on the screen as Olivier speaks them. After the speech, Olivier adds: "This is the story of a man who could not make up his mind." Olivier has often used the "one defect" theory in developing his characterizations for Shakespeare's tragic heroes; he based his notorious *Othello*, for instance, on the notion that the Moor's excessive pride occasioned his downfall. His emphasis of the "one defect" theory in his prologue to *Hamlet*, however, is misleading, as his interpretation of the role is more complex than the simplistic "this is the story of a man who could not make up his mind" would indicate. Olivier felt, though, that it was necessary to give the story an immediate focus for the popular audience.

Taking Olivier at his word, some critics accused him of reducing Shakespeare's most convoluted hero to the most conventional notion of the character's "deficiency." Olivier's performance, in fact, is remarkably varied. Both an ironic observer and a man of action, Olivier's Hamlet is, by fits and starts, embittered, overwrought, speculative, rash, impassioned, withdrawn; like any decent Hamlet, he is a network of contradictions. In her incisive review of the film, Mary McCarthy praised precisely this patchwork quality of Olivier's interpretation, this attempt to avoid a monochromatic reading and to offer instead a portrait of the character that is flamboyant in its "jerkiness," "unsteadiness," hesitations, backtrackings, its periods of immobility followed by irrational bursts of activity: "In any case, this unsteadiness, which is the most striking feature of *Hamlet*, is the thing which most acted versions begin by trying to eliminate, either by 'interpretation' or by a kind of glaze imparted to the diction that makes it (a) inaudible and (b) all of a piece. Sir Laurence Olivier's is the only *Hamlet* which seizes this inconsecutiveness and makes of it an image of suffering, or the failure to feel steadily, to be able to compose a continuous pattern, which is the most harrowing experience of man. Hamlet, a puzzle to himself, is seen by Olivier as a boy, whose immaturity is both his grace and his frailty. The uncertainty as to what is real, the disgust, the impulsiveness, the arbitrary shifts of mood, the recklessness, the high spirits, all incomprehensible in those middle-aged, speechifying Hamlets to whom our stage is habituated, here become suddenly irradiated."[9]

Olivier scrupulously avoids the single-layered approach of many interpretations. Among recent readings, for instance, Richard Burton's (in 1964) was vigorous and assertive, and there was no question of *if* he would seek revenge but *when* he would, whereas Nicol Williamson's Hamlet (in 1969) was a modern neurotic about whom there was every reason to believe that his plans would miscarry. Olivier's character is neither the manipulative, controlling master of ceremonies that Burton's was nor the recessive, paralyzed prince that Williamson portrayed, though his nuanced performance incorporates aspects of both interpretations.

Borrowing ideas, then, from many different approaches to the role, Olivier's Hamlet is many things at once. The actor is careful, however, not to emphasize the rigorous, extroverted, soldierly qualities of the character that would be the easiest for him to play, and he works instead at underlining the meditative qualities, the brooding introspection. He stressses Hamlet's negative traits, his unfitness for heroic action. He is consciously playing against type, making sure that he does not duplicate his performance as Henry V. The result is that the performance, appropriately, is riddled with ambiguity: Is this Hamlet capable of action? Is he really mad or is he only pretending to be?

Inevitably, however, his explosions are more vivid than the passages of philosophical introspection. When he plays the character as a biting, mocking, worldly prince, his performance soars. His stinging closet scene with Gertrude; his leap into Ophelia's grave as he unloads his grief and self-contempt; his frenzied duel with Laertes; his cruel taunting of Ophelia and his baiting of Polonius; his bitter irony before the play-within-the-play interlude—these are the glorious moments when the extroverted actor is truly in his element. It is unfortunate that Olivier eliminated Rosencrantz and Guildenstern because Hamlet's ironic manipulation of his duplicitous friends is exactly the kind of sharp comedy that Olivier excels at.

The dense, interior Hamlet, scorched by self-doubt and existential despair, is intelligent but less effective. The voiceover technique used for the soliloquies prevents the actor from establishing direct communication with the audience. (As Richard III, Olivier smashes film convention by looking directly at the camera—the results are stunning.) Looking like a bronzed matinee idol showing off his profile, Olivier is strangely remote and manneristic in the famous speeches of self-analysis, delivering the character's trimmed soliloquies of despair and irresolution with a distanced recital quality that recalls John Gielgud's attenuated lyricism. Olivier speaks the verse beautifully, however, in measured cadences and with perfect diction. In the 1930s, Olivier had been attacked for his unconventional handling of poetry, for his attempts to turn the verse into naturalistic utterance. In *Hamlet*, there are no traces whatsoever of verbal idiosyncrasy.

Olivier's dyed blond hair, which visually underscores his isolation within the court, also makes his character look decadent. Forty at the time he was playing Hamlet, Olivier is frankly too old for the part, especially in close-ups and especially since Eileen Herlie, his Gertrude, is so youthful-looking. (Herlie was thirty-five.) Olivier had been influenced by Ernest Jones's Freudian analysis of *Hamlet* when he performed the role at the Old Vic in 1937, but in a film intended for general audiences he was initially reluctant to emphasize the character's sexual perversity. Nonetheless, his suggestions of a sensusal, sexually maladjusted Hamlet do color his interpretation, particularly in the forcefully played closet scene where Hamlet straddles Gertrude. This scene, the strongest in the film (played on the queen's enormous, beckoning bed), is acted with marvelous intensity. Olivier reaches a crescendo of frenzy that explodes in his impulsive stabbing of Polonius. Rife with Oedipal overtones, the sexual attachment between Hamlet and Gertrude explains the prince's remarkable animosity to Ophelia; Olivier's fierce denunciation of her in the nunnery scene exposes the character as an entrenched misogynist. Olivier, then, cannot resist playing Hamlet as a sexual neurotic locked in a regressive relationship to Gertrude which causes him to scorn Ophelia's offers of romantic tenderness.

As the director, Olivier took care not to present the play simply as a showcase for a star Hamlet. His performance is not an egocentric display of virtuosity or a blazing rendition of the beleaguered prince. It is, in fact, the least technical and least dazzling of his four major Shakespearean roles on film. By nature, Olivier is more suited to the extroverted heroes like Henry V and Coriolanus and to the parts like Othello and Richard III that allow for elaborate transformations than to the philosophical, dour Hamlet. The character's interiority does not come easily to him, and Hamlet's tragic strain is simply more difficult for the actor to reach than the rich comic possibilities of Richard, the rhetorical skirmishes of Henry, or the melodramatic excesses of Othello. Given the kind of technical actor Olivier is, given his delight in disguise and his method of constructing a character from the outside in, Hamlet could never be his ideal part; and neither his 1937 Hamlet onstage nor his own self-directed performance on film is first-rank Olivier.

Far from indulging himself in a selfish star turn, Olivier shares the frame with his fellow actors. He is particularly yielding and generous in his scenes with Gertrude. There is real electricity in his encounters with this ripe, sensuous queen; Olivier's casting of the young actress was controversial, but Eileen Herlie makes Gertrude wry and alluring. Her potent eroticism makes Hamlet's attachment to her entirely plausible. Their flirtation in court, when Claudius has to shout to separate them, is richly comic. The scenes with

Ophelia are much less forceful. Jean Simmons's Ophelia is by design pale and altogether helpless. Simmons is a colorless actress who had never had any experience in Shakespeare before the film (and has had none since). Because she did not understand the language, she had to be very carefully coached. Vague and puzzled, she is clearly a victim; and her weakness (which comes from the actress herself as well as the character) instigates Hamlet's cruelty. Olivier wanted a shrinking Ophelia to serve as a contrast to his vigorous Gertrude and to highlight Hamlet's tendency to be domineering.

Olivier experimented with unusual concepts for both Gertrude and Ophelia. The remaining interpretations are more conventional. Felix Aylmer is a traditionally befuddled Polonius, all bluster and maddening pomposity. Basil Sydney plays Claudius for human dimension rather than as a grinning Machiavel. He achieves real stature in the prayer scene, thereby stalling Hamlet's plans of revenge. Norman Wooland is an entirely intelligent, sensible Horatio, and he provides therefore a telling contrast to Hamlet's impetuousness.

Although it won the Academy Award as Best Film of the Year, and although Olivier won the Oscar for Best Actor, *Hamlet* was the least critically successful of his three adaptations. In her affirmative review, Mary McCarthy records the popular contemporary objections to the film: " 'You *liked* the Laurence Olivier *Hamlet?*' " breathed a young woman the other day in a shocked undertone, when I mentioned the fact at a party. She herself had not seen the film, the news that it did not employ 'the full resources of the cinema' having reached her in time. 'And I hear Fortinbras has been cut,' she continued, with an inquiring glance into my features, 'not to mention Rosencrantz and Guildenstern. And that the Queen is too young, and the Oedipal theme over-emphasized.' "[10] While some critics thought the film only a photographed play, others attacked it for being too concerned with cinematic virtuosity at the expense of the text: "Olivier. . .in order to allow the camera to play lovingly with all that stonework at Elsinore, all those staircases, the raging sea, and—especially, and oh, so subtly! Gertrude's bed—had to omit about a third of the play."[11]

Within its inevitable limits—Olivier, after all, claimed that this was only a "study" in *Hamlet,* a sketch of the original—the adaptation is a major achievement, providing further demonstration that films can indeed accommodate Shakespeare. In his characteristically sensitive review, James Agee again offers a fitting summation of Olivier's work:

The question used to be: Can Shakespeare's plays be made into successful movies? With his film production of *Henry V* Sir Laurence Olivier settled that question once and for all. But *Henry V* raised another question that it could not answer: Can the screen cope with Shakespeare at his best? Olivier undertook to answer that one, too. . . . The answer is yes. . . . With this admirable filming of one of the most difficult of plays, the whole of Shakespeare's dramatic poetry is thrown wide open to good moviemakers. . . . There can never be a definitive production of a play about which no two people in the world agree. There can never be a thoroughly satisfying production of a play about which so many people feel so personally and so passionately. Very likely there will never be a production good enough to provoke less argument than praise. It can be said of Olivier's version— purely for the sake of argument—that it contains no single unquestionably great performance, but a complete roll call of fine ones: that it is worked with intelligence, sensitivity, thoroughness and beauty; that it has everything which high ambition, deep sobriety and exquisite skill can give it.[12]

5

Richard III

BETWEEN HIS FILMS of *Henry V* and *Hamlet,* Olivier performed with inspiration at the Old Vic. Between *Hamlet* in 1948 and his film adaptation of *Richard III* in 1955, however, his career went into a decline: there were no startling new interpretations during this time, in either theater or films. From March to September of 1948, he toured Australia and New Zealand with the Old Vic, directing himself and Vivien Leigh in *The School for Scandal* and *The Skin of Our Teeth,* and playing Richard III under John Burrell's direction. While on tour, he was informed that he, Ralph Richardson, and John Burrell would not be reappointed as directors of the Old Vic for the following season. The decision of the board was an unpopular one, but the members argued that the celebrity of Olivier and Richardson prevented the two actors from devoting their full attention to the company. At the time of their nonreappointment, Richardson was in Hollywood making a film and Olivier was in Australia, and since receipts at the Old Vic had fallen off, the board was concerned that the theater was becoming too dependent on the box-office value of its illustrious actor-managers. The board did not want the Old Vic to become a star showcase or to compete in terms of glamour with the commercial West End theaters.

Following his dismissal as managing director, Olivier appeared for the company in the 1949 season in London, reviving *The School for Scandal* and *Richard III* and directing Vivien Leigh in an unsuccessful *Antigone.* Olivier's performances at this time were skillful; he was entirely at ease with the brittle style of Sheridan's eighteenth-century comedy of manners, and his Richard was by now like a second skin, but there was little sense of the experimentation and discovery that has always marked his most creative impersonations.

95

Salvador Dali's painting of Olivier as Richard III.

In 1950, after dissolving his association with the Old Vic, Olivier
went into management at the St. James, attempting to restore the
elegant but declining old theater to its former high position. With a
theater of his own at last, Olivier embarked enthusiastically on his
new role of manager. His choice of plays, however, was for the most
part unfortunate, and the number of offerings dwindled sharply
during his sporadic, eight-year tenancy of the theater. His goal at
the St. James was to produce contemporary drama rather than classics, but he never found the combination of important serious drama
with popular appeal that he was looking for. His opening attraction,
a bloated, pretentious blank-verse drama by Christopher Fry called
Venus Observed, with a long, difficult leading role for himself as an
autocratic duke, was prophetic. The play, all but unreadable, has
only a facade of wit and philosophical profundity; and Olivier's
choice of it to inaugurate his management indicated something of his
own predilection for the overblown. A series of now-forgotten titles
followed: *Fading Mansion, Captain Caravallo, Top of the Ladder,
The Happy Time.* His biggest commercial success as producer was
Anastasia; his most adventurous was his presentation (in 1951) of
Orson Welles directing Orson Welles in *Othello.* Olivier's indifferent management of his seasons of modern plays at the St. James was
typical of his relative discomfort with contemporary material.

During this period, Olivier directed two American plays, *Born
Yesterday* (in 1947) and *A Streetcar Named Desire* (in 1949). As
always in dealing with American subjects, his work was unsteady.
He was especially worried that his production of *Streetcar* (in which
he directed Vivien Leigh) was merely an imitation of the acclaimed
New York production of Elia Kazan. Tennessee Williams's play,
with its neurotic heroine, its New Orleans atmosphere, and its encouragement of Method acting, was exactly the sort of material that
Olivier's more external technique was not congenial to. Olivier himself is decidedly not a Williams actor; his recent television performance as Big Daddy in *Cat on a Hot Tin Roof* is certain proof of his
estrangement, in both technique and emotional makeup, from Williams's world of sexual neurotics and misfits. Vivien Leigh, on the
other hand, driven, compulsive, psychotic, with lightning shifts of
mood, was living a life much closer to Blanche du Bois than audiences at the time suspected. As director, Olivier did not interfere
with her remarkable performance, but the production as a whole
lacked the fabled intensity of the Kazan original.

In 1951, for the Festival of Britain, Olivier and Vivien Leigh starred in a season of *Cleopatra* plays. Their wry, high comedy rendition of Shaw's *Caesar and Cleopatra* was well received; their lukewarm *Antony and Cleopatra* was not. In 1953, for the Coronation festivities, he and his wife starred in *The Sleeping Prince*, a slight comedy by Terence Rattigan that Olivier was to direct on film four years later as *The Prince and the Showgirl*. After his electrifying postwar seasons at the Old Vic, and his films of *Henry V* and *Hamlet*, it certainly seemed that in the late 1940s and early 1950s Olivier was simply coasting.

Then, in 1955, in a typical burst of activity and inspiration, Olivier made a splendid film of *Richard III* and had an equally splendid season at the Shakespeare Memorial Theatre in Stratford-on-Avon, offering distinctive interpretations of Malvolio (in *Twelfth Night*), Macbeth, and Titus Andronicus. Peter Brook's Grand Guignol production of Shakespeare's rarely performed, sensational Senecan melodrama developed the kind of exalted reputation that Olivier's double bill of *Oedipus* and *The Critic* had enjoyed a decade earlier: here was theater that dared to be audacious and disrespectful, that risked offending its audience by its display of violent, primitive emotions.

The Third Adaptation

Richard III, Olivier's third Shakespearean film, undertaken after a relatively stale period in his career, is made with wonderful assurance. Olivier's confidence is reflected in the fact that it took him only seventeen weeks to film *Richard* whereas *Hamlet* required six months and *Henry V*, made under difficult conditions during World War II, had absorbed him for an entire year. For the third time, Olivier was working with a crew who understood exactly what he wanted: his production designer was Roger Furse, his art director was Carmen Dillon, his text supervisor was Alan Dent, and the score was again composed by Sir William Walton.

Walton's ceremonial music, and the vivid colors and theatrical stylization of Roger Furse's sets, recall *Henry V*. As in the earlier film, the recurrent tableau effects, the sharp colors and symmetrical compositions, are based on Book of Hours illustrations; the historical drama unfolds before us like a series of pages from an illuminated medieval manuscript. The sets aren't as abstract as those in *Henry*, however, and the film adopts a predominantly uniform style rather than the multi-layered textures used for the earlier work. Castle interiors and the streets of London, though, have the pastel hues of a children's coloring book, and the few landscapes offer a purely decorative and emblematic treatment of physical reality. The film's immaculate fairy-tale world is less exaggerated than that created for *Henry*, less playful and airy, but it is still distinctly theatrical rather than real. As in *Henry*, the film departs from the stylized decor in the climactic battle scene; filmed in Spain, the battle at Bosworth Field takes place on real, parched earth and against a blue sky that moves.

The festive colors and artificial decor used for *Richard III* are less connected to story and characterization than in the first adaptation. Of his three Shakespearean films, in fact, Olivier's *Richard* has the loosest integration between form and content. Shakespeare's melodramatic history play might well have looked less like *Henry V* and more like *Hamlet*. The film's bold colors are pleasing, but how appropriate are they for the story of Richard Crookback's rise and fall? There seems no particular thematic rationale for Richard to hobble through such airy, fanciful settings. Jack J. Jorgens's suggestion that "the artificial set emphasizes the unnaturalness of Richard's actions" is not quite convincing since Olivier doesn't clearly use the pretty sets as an ironic counterpoint to Richard's dark deeds. The sets don't intrude on the story, but they don't enhance it, either: the artful design of the film remains thematically neutral.

As in his two earlier films, Olivier's use of space within the abstract settings is entirely cinematic. Olivier continues here his employment of realist film techniques such as the depth of focus and the long take first fully articulated in *Hamlet*. Scene after scene is composed in eloquent, deep focus, with background details used to comment pertinently on foreground action. Richard and his victims are often in the same frame, separated by arches or platforms or by the vast space of the throne room. Richard often spies on his intended victims from windows or raised galleries; he is dominant in the foreground, hatching his Machiavellian schemes, while his unsuspecting victims are confined to the depth of the frame, often visually enclosed by arches or window bars. As in *Hamlet*, the placement of the characters within the same frame on varying levels and at significant distances from each other provides telling thematic reinforcement. There is a particularly droll use of deep focus when Richard and Buckingham, in the foreground, conspire to murder the young prince, who perches unknowingly on the throne, out of earshot, in the rear of the image. That Richard and Buckingham are themselves separated by a window bar as they confer is a further touch of ironic foreshadowing.

Far more than in *Hamlet,* Olivier here respects the integrity and wholeness of soliloquies and set speeches. In the earlier film, the longer speeches were often presented in a fragmented style, with heavy editing to divide the attention of the audience between the speaker and his environment or his listeners. In *Richard III,* all of the big speeches are filmed in uninterrupted takes so that the actors have the chance to build and shape their delivery without interference from the editor. The sense of flow and of momentum made possible by the long takes is suggested, with spectacular results, by Olivier's opening soliloquy, which is filmed in a single nine-minute take as the actor beckons the camera to follow him around the vast throne room that he plans to claim for himself.

As in *Hamlet,* there are of course scenes in which Olivier departs from the realist methods of deep focus and the long take to use a more hectic and formative approach. This more fragmented style is used for passages of particular theatrical impact, such as the bravura scene in which a series of messengers runs into the throne room to announce to Richard that armies are amassing against him. In this climactic sequence, long shots are punctuated with close-ups; the explosive Eisensteinian editing marks off this passage of the action as special; it is, in fact, the turning point in Richard's fortunes.

As in both *Henry V* and *Hamlet,* Olivier is once again concerned about providing smooth transitions between scenes, about giving the heavily edited and condensed material a sense of continuity and flow. In *Hamlet,* he used a tracking camera to link time and place; here, he uses the less happy device of match cuts, "from the blood running down the axe blade at Hastings' execution to the dripping rag used by a maid to clean some steps, from a bell set wildly spinning by Richard as he slides down the rope to many bells ringing in honor of his coronation, from the blend of blood and wine which flows from the Tower down into the Thames after the murder of Clarence to Mistress Shore placing the King's silver wine pitcher back in its little holy niche."[1]

In a further (and similarly strained) effort to underline thematic connections, Olivier uses two visual leitmotifs, the crown and Richard's shadow. The film begins with a shot of the crown; the scene of Richard's coronation opens with a low-angle shot of a crown that seems suspended in mid-air; at the end of the battle sequence, the crown is trampled under the hooves of horses. The recurrent image of the crown serves as an obvious and unimaginative emblem of kingship and as such the epitome of Richard's aspirations. The use of Richard's shadow, which at one point or another overtakes all the principal characters (most effectively as Richard is about to claim a sexual conquest over Lady Anne) is equally blatant, an example, like the prologue to *Hamlet,* of Olivier's concern for making the material accessible to popular audiences.

The most glaring and ill-considered visual device is the series of superimpositions used to depict Richard's nightmare visions in which he is haunted by the many people he has killed. As Richard lies sleepless in his tent on the eve before Bosworth Field, ghostly apparitions materialize out of and return to the earth, in a jarringly artificial and almost cartoonlike manner that violates the film's sedate visual style.

The strained visual transitions which mar the film represent Olivier's attempts to cover up the many cuts he was forced to make. The job of shaving the play to an acceptable length, and of making the historical details comprehensible to a modern audience, was enormous, an even more difficult assignment in adaptation than *Hamlet.* After he had completed the film in 1955, Olivier told Roger Manvell: "To start with it's a very long play. It's not until the little Princes come on that the story forms that nice river sweep, going swiftly to its conclusion from about half way through the play. The first part up until that moment is an absolute delta of plot and presupposed foreknowledge of events. After all *Richard III* forms the last part of a cycle of four plays, the other three being parts of *Henry VI.* . . . It's a really difficult play to film—it's involved, often obscure. Yet it's always been a popular play—as Dr. Johnson said, its popularity derives from the character of Richard. But I felt it absolutely necessary to do more simplification than I've ever done before, and although every commentator and critic through the centuries had attacked the structure of this play, I quite expect, now, to be accused of vandalism."[2]

Richard III is indeed a cumbersome, awkwardly constructed play, and Olivier's excisions and alterations are for the most part helpful. He eliminates Queen Margaret, widow of King Henry VI, whom Richard has murdered. Margaret, of the House of Lancaster, is both chorus and nemesis, hurling embittered curses at Richard and all the members of his family. Margaret's presence, and her wailing, add a tragic note to the drama, but her hysterical imprecations turn us against Richard, and she would therefore interfere with Olivier's studied attempts to charm us, to make us see the entire action from Richard's point of view. Margaret's speeches enlarge the play thematically and philosophically, but her ringing set speeches are parenthetical to the dramatic action, and Olivier's trimmed version (as in *Hamlet*) concentrates on narrative momentum at the expense of larger historical or political contexts. Olivier also considerably reduces the roles of the other wailing Queens (Elizabeth and the Duchess of York, wife and mother, respectively, to King Edward IV, Richard's father). Elizabeth and the Duchess of York recount the history of the embattled royal families and, like Margaret, are too theatrical, too purely ornamental, for the film's straightforward narrative drive.

Richard's courtship of Lady Anne is divided into two scenes (to increase credibility), though Olivier makes Richard the murderer of Anne's husband, Edward, rather than, as in Shakespeare, of her father-in-law, Henry VI. The character's seduction of Anne, therefore, becomes an act of outrageous daring. Olivier eliminates the long scene where Richard woos Queen Elizabeth for the hand of her daughter; in tone, the courtship simply duplicates Richard's stunt with Lady Anne, and though the encounter affords further evidence of Richard's virtuosity, it is really too much of a good thing. Although he cuts out half-a-dozen characters, he adds a silent Jane Shore, King Edward's mistress, to serve throughout as a token of the corrupt court. He also adds (for the film's opening) the last scene from *Henry VI, Part III*, the coronation of Edward, which introduces all the major characters, provides historical context and continuity, and adds an element of ritual and pageantry which is to figure throughout the film, often in an ironic framework as Richard sets about defiling the Elizabethan concept of the ideal Christian ruler.

Olivier, then, has simplified the structure of Shakespeare's bulky, unevenly balanced play, cutting its choral interludes and its often-wooden rhetorical embellishments and reducing the women's roles in order to concentrate on the main political intrigue of Richard's rise and fall and on his own incomparably witty, incisive, vaudevillian performance.

Olivier as Richard III, savoring his conquest of Lady Anne.

Unlike his earlier adaptations, Olivier here uses the film as a frame for his virtuoso impersonation of Shakespeare's demonic and captivating antihero. The star showcasing is fully earned, however, for with his interpretation of Richard, Olivier is visibly asserting his claim to the title of the world's foremost actor. Every moment of his immense performance is dense and full and surprising. The part of Richard is everything that Olivier could hope for, and it may be that his rendition of Shakespeare's Machiavellian hunchback will be considered his finest work. At the Old Vic after the war, his Richard was his first unmistakably great performance. "I felt complete confidence I'd never felt before," Olivier has said. "I felt what it's necessary for an actor to feel, finally—a little power of hypnotism."[3] Olivier as Richard is a bravura display of a hypnotic actor playing a hypnotic actor, for his king is a sly, droll, resourceful master of the revels who woos and "plays" to the audience, while he manipulates all of the characters in the drama.

On stage, Olivier had enjoyed dressing up for character parts like Justice Shallow, Mr. Puff, Sir Toby Belch, and Julius Caesar, but Richard was his first full-scale disguise on film. (It took him five hours each day to apply his makeup.) With lank, straight black hair, a pointed nose, a hunched back, a pronounced limp, thickened eyebrows, and a pinched, knife-edged nasal voice, Olivier is remarkably transformed. Typically, his performance is coated in externals, and in order to create his vivid effects, he isn't afraid to risk the charge of hamminess or to take Richard to the edge of caricature. Flirting with burlesque exaggeration, he lets us know that he's exulting in the challenges of a virtuoso part. Rather than trying to conceal his technique, the actor proudly flaunts it.

Broad and theatrical as it is, however, the performance has been scaled down for the camera. Using close-ups to establish intimacy with the audience, Olivier takes us into his confidence in a way that would not be available to a stage Richard. He establishes the direct contact with the audience that he so scrupulously avoided as Hamlet; he violates film convention by looking right at the camera, challenging us not to believe him. Olivier claims complete control over both the camera and the audience in the great opening soliloquy,

> Now is the winter of our discontent
> Made glorious summer by this sun of York;
> And all the clouds that lour'd upon our house

In the deep bosom of the ocean buried.
Now are our brows bound with victorious wreaths;
Our bruised arms hung up for monuments;
Our stern alarums chang'd to merry meetings,
Our dreadful marches to delightful measures.
. . . .
But I—that am not shap'd for sportive tricks,
Nor made to court an amorous looking-glass—
I—that am rudely stamp'd, and want love's majesty
To strut before a wanton ambling nymph—
I—that am curtail'd of this fair proportion,
Cheated of feature by dissembling nature,
Deform'd, unfinish'd, sent before my time
Into this breathing world scarce half made up,
And that so lamely and unfashionably
That dogs bark at me as I halt by them—
Why, I, in this weak piping time of peace,
Have no delight to pass away the time,
Unless to spy my shadow in the sun
And descant on my own deformity.

As he roves about the throne room, spitting out his words with succulent irony, the camera moves when and where he wants it to. In hushed, conspiratorial tones laced with self-mockery and self-satisfaction, Richard informs us of his schemes, invites us on as colleagues and well-wishers. The soliloquy is filmed in a single take so there is no intercutting to distract us from what the character says; by the end of the speech, Olivier has us utterly in his power. Throughout the film, he uses asides to the camera as a means of continuing the dialogue he has set up with us. The soliloquies, for the most part, are delivered quietly, with a subtle play of features that wouldn't register on stage: Olivier uses close-ups to show us how Richard thinks.

Richard is an expert dissembler, and it is this aspect of the role that Olivier savors. He plays him as a great comedian, slyly winking at us as he tricks unknowing characters. Early in the film, his courtship of Lady Anne demonstrates Richard's relish for putting on a good show. He plays the wooing scene with calculated impudence, with delight in Richard's persuasive skills; and as he sets out to conquer the lady, whose husband he has killed, Olivier adds a quality that he alone among the great classical actors of his generation is capable of: he makes the hunchback sexy. With Olivier's penetrating eyes and trilling, cooing voice, it's easy to see how Lady Anne is won. The scene is often played for garish comedy, with Anne made up as a painted whore and Richard the most unappealing of would-be lovers, but here the encounter has real sexual tension as Claire Bloom's Anne is a sensuous, dignified lady outwitted by an oddly magnetic suitor.

Olivier underlines the character's mordant wit, emphasizing the discrepancy between what Richard says and what he means, particularly in the scenes where he dissembles before the court as he tries to pass himself off as a retiring person of low ambition who is unskilled with words and unpracticed in political double-dealing. Olivier pitches the ironies directly to us, in order to enlist our sympathy in his pursuits.

The character's greatest acting occurs in the arranged public encounter between him and Buckingham (Ralph Richardson), where he pretends to succumb to the demand for his accession to the throne. Richard enters between two priests, his nose buried ostentatiously in his prayer book. Richard's "performance" takes place on an inner balcony that serves as an appropriately elevated stage. He and Buckingham put on a brilliant show, Buckingham pleading for Richard to assume his lawful claim to the throne, Richard pretending disinterest in worldly matters. When the townspeople accept his refusal and prepare to depart, Richard whispers urgently to his fellow play-actor, "Call them back! Call them back!" After he wins the people over, Olivier throws out his hand for Buckingham to kneel and kiss, and the discordant music, the low-angle shot, Olivier's twisted body and his blazing mocking eyes create an unforgettable image of a crazed tyrant. At this moment of conquest, Richard Crookback is a true grotesque. (Later, in a scene with his innocent young nephews, he has another striking *coup de théâtre;* when the younger of the two princes compares him to an ape, Olivier shoots a look of hatred that is chilling and reptilian.)

Until Richard claims the throne, Olivier's performance is a series of sweeping theatrical gestures that makes us like the character despite ourselves; but once Richard becomes king, the performance becomes darker and more brooding. Olivier drops the wickedly convivial courtship of the audience, and Richard almost seems to lose his sense of humor. The new king seems quite mad, and nowhere is the character's derangement more forcefully demonstrated than in his rejection of Buckingham. In their scenes of political scheming, as Buckingham assists Richard in murdering his way to the throne, Olivier and Ralph Richardson establish a joking, easy relationship, a sense almost of spiritual kinship. When Richard turns on his friend, meeting Buckingham's rightful request for favors with a devastating "I am not in the giving vein today," he seems thoroughly evil.

In the play's final movement, which swiftly charts the haunted king's downfall, Olivier explores the melancholy and doubt that gnaw at the once-confident, once-ebullient Machiavel. Olivier deepens the characterization by removing Richard's mask and allowing us to see the possessed monarch as a pitiful, burnt-out case. The actor doesn't overdo the pathos, however; he doesn't turn Richard into a Christian hero who sees his corruption and repents. Appropriately, even in the king's defeat, Olivier plays for melodrama rather than tragedy. He permits himself a spectacular death scene, Richard's body shaking orgasmically, his sword raised upright in his hand, after a group of soldiers has surrounded him for a ritualistic slaughter. Olivier substitutes this death-as-communal-ritual for the play's hand-to-hand combat between Richard and Richmond.

Olivier, then, despite the darker shadings near the end of the film, plays Richard as a buoyant and richly comic figure. Richard, after all, is not a tragic hero; he is the master of the revels in a rousing, popular, violent melodrama. To sustain the melodramatic flavor of the material, Olivier sees to it that the film has no noble characters (except, briefly, for John Gielgud's Clarence). Claire Bloom's Anne is fatally weak-willed. Cedric Hardwicke plays King Edward as a diseased roué. Richardson's Buckingham is as crafty and sly as Richard, though less ambitious, and therefore less dangerous. The court consists of oily, self-serving politicians, wily double-dealers, or weak, vacillating, easily controlled characters like Edward's wife, Elizabeth. There is no honor here, with Richard and most of his adversaries a collection of ignoble politicians.

As in the two earlier films, the performances have an ensemble consistency. Olivier dominates with a vengeance, controlling the action and the characters, reserving the center of the frame for himself. But the others, especially Ralph Richardson, play opposite him vigorously. The two great actors play Richard and Buckingham like two practiced vaudevillians trading inside information; they make a formidable team, Richardson's calm portrayal of an evil character pointing a contrast to the intoxication with evil of Olivier's Richard. The film offers the additional pleasure of seeing the famed contrast in style between Olivier's rapturous character-acting and his assault on the poetry and Gielgud's lyrical and more remote quality; Gielgud's speeches as the noble Clarence are beautifully "recited." As Kenneth Tynan has written: "John Gielgud is Kemble to Olivier's Kean—the aesthete, as opposed to the animal. 'John is claret,' as Alan Dent once put it, 'and Larry is burgundy.' The difference between them reminds me more of Edmund Burke's famous essay on the Sublime and the Beautiful. According to Burke's definition, the Beautiful (i.e. Gielgud) comprises that which is shapely, harmonious and pleasing; while the Sublime (i.e. Olivier) is irregular, jagged and awe-inspiring, like thunder over the Matterhorn."[4]

Richard III received the most glowing reviews of the three adaptations. There was, by this time, and because of Olivier's two earlier successes, almost no resistance to the idea of putting Shakespeare on film. Bosley Crowther, in the *New York Times,* summed up critical and popular opinion when he wrote, "The measure of Sir Laurence Olivier's genius for putting Shakespeare's plays on the screen is beautifully and brilliantly exhibited in his production and performance of Richard III."[5]

Shakespeare on Film without Olivier

The popular and critical success of *Henry V, Hamlet,* and *Richard III* has inspired only a handful of other Shakespearean adaptations. Among English-language productions, Orson Welles's *Macbeth* (1947), *Othello* (1951), and *Chimes at Midnight [Falstaff]* (1965), Franco Zeffirelli's *Taming of the Shrew* (1967) and *Romeo and Juliet* (1968), Joseph Mankiewicz's *Julius Caesar* (1953), and Peter Brook's *King Lear* (1971) have been outstanding; among foreign-language versions, Lev Kosintsev's Russian *Hamlet* (1964) and Akira Kurosawa's 1957 Japanese *Throne of Blood* (based very loosely on *Macbeth)* have been especially well received. While each of these major adaptations has individual virtues, none has achieved the same blend of excellence of performance, fidelity to text, and sophistication of film techniques as Olivier's three landmark productions.

Welles's films of *Macbeth* and *Othello* served as showcases for the director's celebrated baroque style. Both adaptations are filled with striking compositions in depth and shadow, with low-angle shots that distort figures and landscape, with creative sound effects that sometimes take precedence over the language. The films are a succession of virtuoso moments like the long tracking shot on the ramparts in *Othello* and the expressionistic montage sequence that opens *Macbeth*. Welles, typically, was working on limited budgets, and, also typically, almost succeeded in disguising that fact. His *Macbeth*, made on a shoestring for Republic Studios, an outfit best known for its series of modest westerns, creates for the play an effectively primitive environment. The action takes place in a palace that looks like a prehistoric cave. Its subterranean rooms are made of rocklike formations that ooze water, the dripping of which acts as an aural accompaniment to some of Macbeth's interior monologues. The harsh, barren world the film presents looks like the projection of Macbeth's tortured spirit; as in Olivier's *Hamlet*, and in Peter Brook's stark *King Lear*, set in a severely parched and unaccommodating landscape, Welles uses scenic design as a reflection of his protagonist's state of mind. The bare world of Welles's *Macbeth* is governed by dark and unknowable fates rather than by a Christian God.

As in his other two adaptations—and more extensively than Olivier—Welles cuts and rearranges the text; we seem to be getting a skeletal version of Shakespeare's original material. And the acting in these films is either indifferent (Jeanette Nolan's Lady Macbeth, for instance) or (like Jeanne Moreau's forlorn, sagging Mistress Quickly in *Chimes at Midnight*) glaringly inadequate. Despite his magnificent voice, Welles himself is not an interesting Shakespearean actor. His interpretations of Macbeth, Othello, and especially Falstaff are surprisingly lackluster. His Macbeth and Othello are rendered with a traditional recital (almost singsong) quality, while his Falstaff attempts a daring revaluation of the character by presenting him not as a jolly maker of mayhem, not as a robust figure of misrule and disorder, not, in short, as conventionally Falstaffian, but as moody and melancholy, a gross and saturnine clown. The result is dank and lifeless, however, rather than revelatory.

Zeffirelli's *Taming of the Shrew* and *Romeo and Juliet* offer luxuriously realistic recreations of Renaissance Italy. In gorgeous color and to the strains of lush scores, Zeffirelli's camera caresses the costumes and the architecture of a meticulously rendered Renaissance decor. These films have the sense of real space and architectural solidity that Olivier never strove for and that he proved are not necessary for giving Shakespeare filmic dimensions. In order to concentrate on the richly detailed atmosphere, Zeffirelli strips Shakespeare's plays to an inescapable minimum. His actors—inexperienced youngsters, in the case of *Romeo and Juliet,* and Richard Burton and Elizabeth Taylor, the reigning movie stars in the world at the time, for *Shrew*—are cast for their visual appeal rather than (except for Burton) their Shakespearean training. The results, though, are marvelous: Shakespeare is popularized for movie audiences in entirely acceptable ways. The spirit if not always the language of Shakespeare's romantic tragedy and rousing comedy of the battle between the sexes is preserved. Leonard Whiting and Olivia Hussey, as the passionate, young Romeo and Juliet, and the Burtons as Petruchio and Katharine, perform with enormous flair and charm. Zeffirelli, then, approaches Shakespeare's plays not as if they were inviolate sacred text, but as the basis for popular movies that feature swirling movement, a kaleidoscope of rich colors and designs, and romantic music. His *Romeo* is the most financially successful of all film adaptations of Shakespeare. Zeffirelli's extraordinarily textured films, feasts for the eye and ear, would surely have pleased Shakespeare, himself a practical man of the theater and a popular writer.

Joseph Mankiewicz's *Julius Caesar* steers a sober middle ground between Welles's ornate stylization and Zeffirelli's free-wheeling cinematic realism. It is the single Shakespearean film produced by a major Hollywood studio with an all-star cast of film actors (Marlon Brando, James Mason, Louis Calhern, Edmond O'Brien, Greer Garson, Deborah Kerr, Edmund Purdom—only John Gielgud, playing Cassius, was a classical actor) that satisfied both Shakespearean scholars and general audiences. Never flashy, its sense of place at once real and specific, the film is firmly acted, intelligently and sensibly directed. *Julius Caesar* had long first-run, reserved-seat engagements in major cities and even realized a modest profit for its studio, Metro-Goldwyn-Mayer: Why haven't there been more films like it?

6

Filmed Theater

EXCEPT, BRIEFLY AND GLORIOUSLY, with his triumphant *Henry V*, Olivier was never a dominant force in the British film industry. As an actor, he moved freely between British and American films, always available for small parts in big pictures, big parts in small ones, and big parts in big ones. As a director, however, his opportunities were limited by financial considerations. He attributes Alexander Korda's untimely death, in 1957, to his inability to finance a long-planned film of *Macbeth*. Korda had produced *Richard III*, and Olivier feels the film could never have been made, certainly not with the style and gloss it had, if Korda had not supervised the project. Olivier and Korda had planned a similar collaboration at the time of the producer's death. Olivier took his proposal to other producers, but at the time contemporary realistic subjects were the vogue; no one was interested in financing the film, despite the fact that Olivier's track record with Shakespeare was remarkable: all three of his adaptations had made money.

Olivier was so dejected by his failure to sell *Macbeth* that he has never tried since to undertake another full-scale adaptation. He has directed only two films since *Richard III—The Prince and the Showgirl* (1957) and *Three Sisters* (1970). In both cases (as in his Shakespearean films), he was directing himself in material that he had first performed on the stage, but in both later films he concentrated on acting as opposed to visual design and fluency. *The Prince and the Showgirl* and *Three Sisters* are much more vulnerable to the charge of "filmed theater" than his Shakespearean productions.

Since *Richard III*, Olivier has appeared on film and on television in several classic plays in which he had had conspicuous success on stage. The film versions of these acclaimed performances—*Othello* (1966), *Uncle Vanya* (1964), *The Dance of Death* (1969), *Long Day's*

111

Olivier as Othello (1966).

Journey into Night (1973), and *The Merchant of Venice* (1973)—
were made as permanent records of Olivier's achievements rather
than as fully conceived films. These straightforward transcriptions of
stage productions therefore lack the richness and sense of wholeness
of Oliver's great adaptations.

In the films of *Uncle Vanya*, *Othello*, and *The Dance of Death*,
the action is set against antinaturalistic backgrounds that are clearly,
and without apology, stage sets. In his three adaptations, Olivier
had never denied or tried to conceal the theatrical derivation of his
material—that would have been impossible, anyway—but even to
emphasize it, while at the same time to suggest in his use of space
the openness of the film frame rather the closed, centripetal impact
of the stage picture. In his penetrating essays on theater and film in
What Is Cinema?, Andre Bazin underlines the differences between
theatrical space and film space. Theatrical space, he suggests, is
closed off from the world outside the theater and separated by foot-
lights from the audience. Space on a stage is precisely delimited,
contained by the circumference of a spotlight. Space in film is
open-ended; the film frame is a window on the world. Bazin writes:
"The stage and the decor where the action unfolds constitute an
aesthetic microcosm inserted perforce into the universe but essentially distinct from the Nature which surrounds it. It is not the same
with cinema, the basic principle of which is a denial of any frontiers
to action. . . . 'The theatre,' says Baudelaire, 'is a crystal chan-
delier.' If one were called upon to offer in comparison a symbol
other than this artificial crystal-like object, brilliant, intricate, and
circular, which refracts the light which plays around its center and
holds us prisoners of its aureole, we might say of the cinema that it is
the little flashlight of the usher, moving like an uncertain comet
across the night of our waking dream, the diffuse space without
shape or frontiers that surrounds the screen."[1]

Bazin notes that theatrical space focuses almost exclusively on the
actor while films insist on the interaction between the actor and the
setting. How space is filled is crucial in films, whereas the theater
can survive with the actor abandoned against a blank background.
Even stylized films with unrealistic settings must create a realistic
sense of space.

Olivier's Shakespearean films place actors within the openness of
cinematic space and therefore avoid the charge of being merely
filmed theater, while the later, minimalist films confine the actors to

the closed, static frame of the theater, placing them within the circumference of a metaphorical if not always an actual spotlight.

The Prince and the Showgirl

Unlike *Three Sisters* and the films made simply as records of Olivier's famous stage performances, *The Prince and the Showgirl* is played in realistic settings. There is nothing in the film's visual design to set it apart from conventional Hollywood realism. Yet the material, with its confined drawing-room setting and its artificial storyline, looks unmistakably like a theater piece transported uncomfortably to an alien and resistant medium.

In 1956, after his third successful screen adaptation of Shakespeare, Olivier was thoroughly enchanted with film direction, and he was interested in trying other kinds of material besides the Bard. For his first (and, unfortunately, his only) film version of popular material, he selected Terence Rattigan's *The Sleeping Prince*, in which he had appeared on stage with Vivien Leigh. Rattigan wrote the play as an occasional piece to celebrate Queen Elizabeth's coronation, and the story, about an encounter between a Transylvanian prince and an American showgirl that takes place in 1911 when international royalty gathered in London for the coronation of King George V and Queen Mary, is indeed slight. Rattigan himself has described the plot as "frail practically to the point of invisibility." The busy, unromantic prince, whom Rattigan intended as a Prince Uncharming, finds a chorus girl but discovers that if "she is going to be seduced at all, it must be to the accompaniment of *tzigane* music, quotations from *Antony and Cleopatra*, and dialogue about her eyes being like 'twin pools' and her hair being like 'spun gold.' . . . Hating himself, he provides the *tzigane* music and says all the expected words; but then, to his horror and anguish, he finds that she has taken them seriously and has decided to stay with him not for an hour but for life. His frenzied attempts to disentangle himself from this imbroglio thereafter make the whole play, together with his genuine transformation from Prince Uncharming, if not into Prince Charming, at least into Prince Half-Way-Human. . . . I meant it purely as a little nonsense for a great occasion."[2]

Rattigan decidedly did not want the Oliviers to star in it as he felt they were too imposing for his fluff; he feared that their illustrious presence might give the production a stature he didn't feel was at all warranted. Olivier was intrigued by the part, however, and he insisted on directing and starring in the play. With his accent, his imperial manner, his temperamental rages, and his predilection for turning politics and romance into play-acting, the prince is the kind of theatrical personality that Olivier has always relished. And the good-hearted showgirl who awakens the prince and even forestalls a palace revolution seemed in prospect an equally challenging role for Vivien Leigh. In the 1953 London production, Leigh, however, was too delicate and genteel for Rattigan's dizzy Brooklyn chorus girl, and when Olivier decided to adapt the play into a film, he realized that he would have to cast the showgirl with a real American. He selected the most famous American showgirl in the world: Marilyn Monroe. At the time (1956), Monroe was not the transcendental figure she has become since her death, and skeptics thought Olivier was slumming. "What could the great tragedian, the dean of English actors, have in common with the Yankee lass, the dean of American blondes, who is known mainly for inventing perpetual motion?" asked the gossip columnists. But Olivier's casting was absolutely correct, of course—Monroe was ideal for embodying Rattigan's innocent, wistful heroine.

There were rumors of disputes and tantrums on the set. Before she went to London, Marilyn had been studying at the Actors Studio and Paula Strasberg, wife of Lee Strasberg, director of the Studio, was onhand as a coach-in-residence. Olivier has never had patience for Method naturalism, and he couldn't understand Marilyn's constant need to discuss motivation. His own technique, proceeding from outside in, clashed with Monroe's interior approach; they built their characterizations in exactly opposite ways. Olivier had been prepared to make concessions because he had been warned that his costar was seriously troubled; but he was not willing to pamper unduly what he regarded as a wrong-headed, self-indulgent approach to acting, nor did he feel he had to put up with Marilyn's tardiness, her downright rudeness to cast and crew, her vulgarity and monstrous selfishness. It was impossible for them to become friends, but the two performers play beautifully together, and the obvious difference in their style of performance enhances the thin material.

The showgirl has the instinct and the childlike emotions that confirm our view of what the real-life Monroe must have been like, while the prince has the calculated mask that suggests Olivier's highly technical and external approach to constructing a character.

Though it is the result of overwrought study and psychotic insecurity, Marilyn's work seems effortless, her own being welded inseparably to that of her character. She is a star who holds us by the charm of her personality, whereas Olivier is an actor whose own presence we hardly glimpse beneath the glasses, the whiskers, and the accent of the prince.

Significantly, Olivier is all dressed up for his part while Monroe wears a simple white dress that reveals every curve and bulge of her

The Prince and the Showgirl (1957): Olivier "all dressed up," Marilyn Monroe "in a simple white dress."

figure. As a naive, charming, but sly showgirl, Marilyn is playing
what the audience assumes is an extension of herself. Moviegoers
could not distinguish between her on-screen and off-screen personae, between the public and the private Marilyn, and perhaps
neither could she. With Olivier, of course, it was not possible to
make the same easy connection between the actor and his role, for
we had no idea of what he was really like when he wasn't playing a
part. Though, clearly, he was not simply playing himself as the
prince, we could not tell how much of his own personality he was
using: as always, the man was buried in the character. Monroe's
timing, her reactions, all seem the result of inspired instinct,
whereas Olivier works studiously to achieve his effects. In his or her
own style, each is splendid.

Olivier's part is showier, more difficult and technical than Monroe's, as it calls for an accent, and is studded with temperamental
explosions. The prince is a poseur, a ham actor, a phony; and typically, Olivier is not interested in whether or not he "tarnishes" his
image by playing an unsympathetic character. Presenting the prince
as a stubborn, brittle, petty tyrant, Olivier attacks the role without
regard for risking our displeasure, and yet he is never so heavy that
he obscures the character's charm or, as Rattigan feared, dismantles
the lightweight story.

Olivier does a great deal of acting in the film, but, as both director
and costar, he gallantly hands the film to his leading lady, allowing
her many special moments that turn *The Prince and the Showgirl*
into something of an homage to Marilyn Monroe. The film is
punctuated with little set pieces that display Monroe's particular
gifts as a light comedienne and as a sentimental actress. While the
Regent is jabbering on the phone, preoccupied with affairs of state
and with court intrigue, and thoroughly insensitive to the girl's
presence, the camera lingers on Monroe as she helps herself to hors
d'oeuvres and reacts, a little drunkenly, to the prince's tactless
comments about Americans. The scene is beautifully timed, and
Olivier discovers an easy, sly sense of humor in his costar. In the
coronation scene, the camera focuses on Monroe as she reacts to the
splendor of the royal ceremony; the scene is a showcase for the
childlike innocence and trembling vulnerability that Marilyn's audience always responded to. Olivier provides Monroe with a magnificent exit: the camera remains in place as Marilyn leaves the royal
apartments; at the end of her long walk through the ornate rooms,

she nods to the liveried footman just before she passes out of view, into the outside world, and that small, marvelously apt gesture perfectly summarizes the character's charm and dignity.

The wallbound material doesn't have the opportunity for spectacle, for movement, and for changes of scene that the Shakespearean plays afforded, and Olivier's direction (wisely, under the circumstances) is less inventive than in any of his earlier projects. He treats the text as a duet for two accomplished light comedians, concentrating on matters of acting, on timing, nuance, gesture, rather than on visual adornment. Olivier uses unobtrusive camera movement and editing and minimal changes of scene to give some fluidity to the circumscribed material. The film opens with a charming backstage sequence where the prince is hastily introduced to the vague, tardy showgirl (an in-joke on Monroe's famed lateness?). The scene at her boardinghouse of her frantic preparations for her evening with the regent is also a delightful embellishment of the play's single drawing-room set; but later interpolations are less successful. The scenes at the coronation and the ball are filmed in a skimpy way that suggests a modest budget. The royal procession through the streets and in Westminster Abbey seems posed; the sense of space is cramped. It looks as if Olivier is faking it, and the entire sequence, while it breaks up the single-set confinement, has a theatrical rendering of physical reality that is jarring. Olivier works best in the interior scenes, where he can focus on acting, rather than in the big crowd scenes, where his direction is surprisingly stilted. When it strays from the story's theatrical confinement, when it ventures out into the "real" world, the picture is suspended uncomfortably in an undefined space between theatrical convention and cinematic realism.

Despite its extraordinary casting, *The Prince and the Showgirl* was not popular, nor has it since its initial release acquired a cult reputation. Audiences have never really taken to it, perhaps because it is genuinely stagy, claustrophobic, arch—the material never quite manages to move comfortably within the film frame.

Chekhov, Strindberg, and O'Neill on Film

Unlike *The Prince and the Showgirl*, Olivier's *Three Sisters* and the films made to preserve his stage performances make no attempt whatsoever to conceal their theatrical origins; these transcriptions make minimal concessions to the film medium. *Three Sisters, Uncle*

Vanya, The Dance of Death, and *Long Day's Journey into Night* are set in environments that are intentionally claustrophobic, and for the films to have opened up the material, to have expanded the number of settings and to have introduced exterior locations would have been gratuitous. But the films use their intentionally limited space in theatrical rather than cinematic ways.

These closed, classically constructed plays, with their compressed time spans and their severely limited settings, are entirely different from the exuberant open-form romanticism of Shakespeare's methods, and they require a different kind of cooperation from the sympathetic film adapter, one attuned to nuances of mood and atmosphere. All four plays are realistic portraits of doomed characters. The movement of the dramas is inward, as the characters tear away at each other—quietly, subtly, indirectly, in the case of Chekhov, explosively in the case of Strindberg and O'Neill. These are plays for actors, but on film the actors need to be placed in a more full-bodied environment than the bare films offer; without the cinematic framing, the performances, acclaimed on the stage, seem curiously external and technical, with the close-up camera seeming to expose the actors' methods; we are too aware of "performance."

It isn't so much that the performances, conceived originally for the theater, are uncomfortable on film because they have not been scaled down to accommodate the probing camera, though this problem of adjustment of size is apparent at times, as that the actors are abandoned against blank backgrounds, against a dead space that is theatrical rather than cinematic. We can almost see the greasepaint and feel the presence offstage of wings and dressing-rooms, whereas in films the illusion of reality ought to stretch beyond the frame. There is no ongoing flow of life in these films, no sense that what we are seeing is connected to reality. The movement in these films is stiff, frozen, as if prearranged: we are seeing images composed for the stage onto which the syntax of film has been uncomfortably grafted.

The films are awkwardly edited, so that scenes are often fragmented in order to focus only on the actor who is speaking, whereas the real drama in each of the plays is in the coiled interconnections among groups of characters. The thematic and visual center in all four plays is in configurations of embattled characters rather than in isolated characters delivering monologues. The intercutting, which separates individual characters and splinters the action into choppy bits and pieces, impedes the sense of group dynamics which is crucial to the plays. As opposed to the fractured editing style, the films need a greater sense of spatial and temporal integrity made possible through long takes, depth of field, and the moving camera. With their skeletal sets, which abandon the actors in unlocalized space, and their disruptive and indiscriminate pattern of intercutting, the films of *Uncle Vanya, Three Sisters, The Dance of Death,* and *Long Day's Journey into Night* undermine the effectiveness of the actors.

Directed by Stuart Burge, *Uncle Vanya* is a transcription of a highly praised stage production starring Olivier, Michael Redgrave, Joan Plowright, Rosemary Harris, and Sybil Thorndike. Olivier's performance as Astrov has been called his finest repertory work. With beautiful understatement, he captures the doctor's cynicism and carelessness, his lazy sensuality, his boredom. Detached, preoccupied, he yet suggests the character's underlying romanticism. Beneath the doctor's present slothfulness, Olivier indicates that there was once a handsome ladies' man as well as an idealist in love with a dream of reclaiming the Russian forests. Olivier's subtle, complex performance, totally stripped of spectacular effects, silenced critics who traditionally decried his repertory appearances as too explosive and self-serving. With a proper sense of Chekhovian balance, then, Olivier presents Astrov as both idealist and cynic, as a once-dashing gentleman now gone quietly to seed. Instead of observing Chekhov's own detachment and thereby allowing the drama to unfold from a distance that permits us to observe groups of characters as they interact, Burge uses a jagged editing style that often isolates Olivier and the other actors within their own space. The film's punctuation underlines the fact that we are watching Olivier, star actor, when in fact Olivier is giving an ensemble performance that has absolutely none of the dazzle, none of the emphatic technique, that he uses when he is attacking a big starring role. Astrov is not the leading role—there are no leading roles in Chekhov, when his work is being properly performed. Burge's indifferent filming does not erase the immense subtlety of Olivier's performance but it fails to place it within a group setting that would enhance its wonderfully yielding, blended quality.

Except for Olivier and Michael Redgrave, as an intensely self-pitying Uncle Vanya, the other actors are not experienced film performers; their delivery is not only keyed to the stage but their precise enunciation is more appropriate to Shakespeare than to the casual, easy, natural rhythms of Chekhov's colloquial language. The English always approach Chekhov as though he were in fact Shakespeare; this production, too, suffers from its reverence. Chekhov is being played too stiffly and properly; there is too much declamation here, when Chekhov's sad, bemused characters are only speaking quietly among themselves. The film's visual stiffness is thus reinforced by the actors' elocutionary mode which (with the exceptions of Olivier and Redgrave) encloses them as characters in a play rather than as people in a world on film.

Produced six years after this very spare *Uncle Vanya*, *Three Sisters* is a more fluent adaptation. Olivier's direction contains genuine attempts to move the material gracefully from behind the proscenium, but nonetheless this is by far his least cinematic work. Like *Uncle Vanya*, *Three Sisters* concerns a group of characters who feel they have wasted their lives. The eponymous sisters are trapped in a provincial town while longing to go to Moscow; their dream of Moscow becomes an emblem of human aspiration that is doomed to failure and frustration. The three sisters are tokens of a cultivated aristocracy that is being gradually erased by a grasping bourgeoisie, represented in the play by the vulgar Natasha, who marries Andrei, the sisters' brother, and who systematically dispossesses the sisters of their home. In her rapacity and greed, Natasha is a sharp contrast to the fineness and even, despite their inertia, the nobility of the sisters. There are no heroes or villains in Chekhov, though, since the playwright views his characters with an objectivity that confers humanity on all of them.

Olivier begins the film with a stunning shot of Chekhov's heroines glimpsed in silhouette behind a shimmering, scrimlike partition. The camera tracks in step with the sisters as they move sedately in single file through the vast empty space of their provincial house. The compositional quality of the opening announces Olivier's dependence on theater—the characters' ritualistic movement, the artificial backlighting that frames them, the unoccupied space, are means equally available to the stage director. The sisters' house looks like a stage set, its large rooms decorated with only a few pieces of antique furniture; and the garden and surrounding forest used for the last act are decidedly artificial. Olivier has excluded the world of physical reality, choosing instead to enclose the characters in theatrical settings that are both two- and three-dimensional.

Weather, natural light, realistic sense of space, naturalistic decor—these are rigorously omitted from the film's spare design.

Olivier tiptoes in hushed tones through a play that he has called "the most beautiful in the world," and as a result his direction is more solemn and stately than it was for his Shakespearean adaptations. Olivier is not intimidated by Shakespeare; on the evidence of this film, he *is* afraid of Chekhov. His approach is too muted and remote, and his direction lacks the energy that propelled the Shakespearean films.

Chekhov presents his characters as they function in society—their private dramas of unrequited love, of regret for missed or wasted opportunities, are enacted in public, on lawns, in living rooms, where there is a continual coming and going of people. Chekhov's plays are composed of a series of group portraits; and films, which by tradition (though not by necessity) break up conversations into two-shots, or close-ups, only destroy the rhythm of the scenes. *Three Sisters*, like *Uncle Vanya*, is written for the unbroken, unfragmented movement of actors on a stage. Realizing this, Olivier uses the camera as little and as quietly as possible; he tries, more than Burge in *Uncle Vanya*, to include many group shots, and to depend on neutral medium shots that do not divide the audience's attention from the group interrelationships. Olivier uses close-ups sparingly, for emphasis. Despite his comparative discretion, however, the Act I dinner party, for instance, is not nearly so effective on film as it is on stage; the sense of ensemble movement and of simultaneous activity, which often has an exhilarating spontaneity and lifelikeness in the theater, is missing here. The flow of life, so essential to Chekhov's mood and rhythm, is dissipated by Olivier's too-careful arrangement of actors for the camera.

Chekhov balances the tone and mood of his four acts; the scenes are arranged in complementary pairs, so that the high spirits of the Act I party are followed by the gloomy, isolated conversations of Act II; the excitement instigated by the offstage fire in Act III is balanced by the somber leavetakings in Act IV. Olivier's direction is dark and heavy from the beginning, however; this is a stern, elegiac reading of the play that misses some of the humor (Chekhov thought of his plays as comedies, and he objected to Stanislavsky's sentimentalization of the original productions). Olivier's reverential approach downplays the festive atmosphere of the Act I dinner and the nervous energy occasioned by the offstage fire in Act III. The film's

courtesy American Film Theatre

Olivier as Dr. Chebutykin with Joan Plowright as Masha in Chekhov's *Three Sisters*
(1970)

stately pace is unbroken except for superfluous interjections of a fire truck hurtling through a city street and an impressionistic dream sequence of two of the sisters wandering around a fogbound Moscow that they will never reach. Both these naive attempts to expand the material betray the film's otherwise deliberately confined atmosphere. These two brief intrusions are failures of judgment unprecedented in Olivier's film-directing.

Most of his actors (recruited from his National Theatre production) do not carry over to film the kind of presence and authority they have onstage. They are all technically proficient, but they are a little cool for Chekhov. The film has a staid drawing-room atmosphere that belies Chekhov's palpitating, reverberent subtext. Only Joan Plowright's Masha (the most intensely unhappy of the sisters, trapped in a marriage to a dull, well-meaning schoolteacher) and Alan Bates's Vershinin (a soldier, also trapped in a loveless marriage) suggest the coiled, highstrung temperaments of Chekhov's characters. The scenes of their brief romance, in which Masha's embittered realism brushes against Vershinin's romanticism, are taut and incisive. The only other performance that captures the Chekhovian tension between casual surface and urgent subtext is Olivier's cameo of the self-pitying, irascible, drunken doctor, Chebutykin.

The 1963 Actors Studio production of the play, directed by Lee Strasberg, was more manneristic and self-indulgent than Olivier's controlled film, but also more distinctive, more dynamic. Strasberg's Method-trained actors (Shirley Knight, Kim Stanley, Barbara Baxley, Geraldine Page), employing the traditional stammers, repetitions, and backtrackings, released the tension and dissatisfaction of Chekhov's characters more forcefully than Olivier's company. The American actors caught the characters' languor and bitterness, their caustic humor, their neuroses, whereas the sedate and too-well-behaved British company remained for the most part on the periphery of the drama. Stanislavski created his System as a means of excavating Chekhov's internalized characters; and the Method, which is the New York adaptation of the System, is more useful in probing Chekhov than the classical training of the National Theatre actors.

Olivier's film has a beautifully muted color scheme—rich browns and velvets, weighty dark tones for the interiors, with sharply contrasted lighting, and a gray, Corotlike, autumnal atmosphere for the last-act farewells in the garden. The film is intelligent, (too) dignified, and never fully moving. Even more than *The Prince and the Showgirl*, it looks like a filmed play rather than a full-fledged movie.

Olivier's performance as the Captain in Strindberg's *Dance of Death*, at the National Theatre in 1967, was one of the most spectuacular of his career, and he agreed, reluctantly, to record the performance on film. *The Dance of Death*, a naturalistic play hurled out of Strindberg's depths in the middle of his expressionist period, was written in 1901 (the same year as *Three Sisters*), when Strindberg was fifty-two. The tortured playwright had already weathered two savage marriages, and he was about to embark on a third and final marriage that would also turn out to be disastrous. A partial reflection of Strindberg's first marriage, to the actress Siri von Essen, the husband and wife in *The Dance of Death* thrive on their hatred for each other and on their intense self-loathing. In Strindberg's marriage pit, cruelty, rage, tyranny, paranoia are signs of vitality. The Captain and his wife, Alice, are most truly in possession of themselves when they are aiming for the kill, when they are vampires, determined on sucking the blood out of their mates. In the hell that is their marriage, to be most creative is to discover ways of knocking one's opponent to the mat. In their compulsive dance to the death, their timing is superb, their pace giddy. It's push and shove, thrust and counterthrust, right up to the final ghastly moment, when, at last, the Captain drops dead, thereby fulfilling his wife's greatest wish. In Strindberg's marital madhouse, chaos yields ultimately to resolution: the characters are finally saved because they know how to dramatize their feelings.

"People don't do such things," Judge Brack says at the end of Ibsen's *Hedda Gabler* when the distraught heroine finally puts a bullet through her head, and we might as well apply the same reservation to Strindberg's characters. The conflicts in *The Dance of Death* are larger than life—they're too grand and too simplified—yet they are not unlike life. Through his two characters, Strindberg dramatized his own attraction to intense feelings; in his own excruciating self-torture and in his sadistic laceration of others he found vitality and sustenance. Like his characters, too, Strindberg was something of a poseur. Transferring his agony from life to art, he institutionalized his suffering. In the late nineteenth century, at the tag end of the Romantic tradition, it was fashionable for a great artist to be mad; being crazy certified your claim to genius, and playing up the role of the madman genius was, after all, profitable. It was a way of holding on to celebrity and it was a kind of self-celebration.

Strindberg was doubtless a prime candidate for the analyst's couch, but he wasn't so disturbed that he couldn't convert his demons into art. His husband and wife in *The Dance of Death* too are wildly disturbed, but they also qualify as marvelous performers. The Captain and Alice warm to an audience. When an old friend comes to visit, they are primed to put on a show. Consummate actors, they're "up" whenever they have an observer. Being "mad" for them, as probably for Strindberg, is not more than they can handle. Living before the age of psychiatry, Strindberg went to art rather than to doctors to cure himself, and what a relief it must have been for him to create in this play this ugly, bickering, malevolent, finally rather glorious and even saved couple—the lordly preening paranoid Captain and his gross and saintly Alice.

The Captain is obviously a role tailor-made for Olivier. His embittered, venomous Captain, always coiled like a cobra for a poisonous assault on his wife, is a performance of operatic expansiveness. In its high voltage, its risks, its breathtaking leaps of pitch and volume, the Captain is a companion piece to his Othello; like the Moor, Strindberg's wildly neurotic character releases Olivier's own bottled-up violence. The cramped film, with its perfunctory editing and camera work, doesn't allow Olivier's grand performance to breathe fully. Playing the Captain's rages and eruptions at full volume, Olivier gives the camera more than it can absorb comfortably—the camera pushes him into corners and exposes his "acting." The performance looks like a transplantation from the theater, but it contains heady intimations of the actor's grandeur in a bravura role ideally suited to his histrionic temperament, and it is a valuable record of one of his highest achievements.

Olivier's overtly theatrical performance in *Long Day's Journey into Night* (a television production of another acclaimed National Theatre presentation) is also justified by the material; as in *The Dance of Death*, he is again playing a self-dramatizing character. (In its psychic conflicts, its titanic anger, and its concentrated form, *The Dance of Death* is in fact the prototype for O'Neill's play, as it is also for another great American drama of family warfare, Edward Albee's *Who's Afraid of Virginia Woolf?*) Like the Captain, the patriarch in *Long Day's Journey* is something of a poseur, a ham actor who is onstage even when he is sitting at home with his family. James

Tyrone acts as if he is one of the larger-than-life romantic heroes he built his career in playing. A once-promising classical actor who sacrificed his art for popular and commercial success in *The Count of Monte Cristo*, Tyrone is a second-rater, and he knows it; his high-toned manner is a bluff that Olivier exposes, just as his hunched posture, his sour expression, his air of defeat and disappointment convey the character's self-estimate. Olivier's theatrical accent, tinged with phoniness, reveals the character's use of performance to protect him from confronting the truth about his failed career and his disastrous marriage to a once-lovely woman now addicted to drugs. Like all the members of this tortured household (based on O'Neill's own family), Tyrone cannot live with the truth—his affected manner, his play-acting, is a way of distancing himself from grim reality. Because an emphatic approach reveals the essence of this failed, flailing patriarch, Olivier can get away with not subduing his immense performance for the television cameras.

Othello and *The Merchant of Venice*

Olivier's Othello and his Shylock were recorded on film (Othello for a limited two-day booking in film theaters throughout the country in 1966; Shylock for a television production in 1973) not only because they were two of his most daring interpretations but because of popular demand for making the performances accessible to larger audiences than would have been able to see them at the National. These two performances are splendid examples of Olivier's late classical manner, and it is appropriate that they are therefore preserved on film, as a permanent record of the fully ripened technique of the century's preeminent classical actor.

Both performances are coated with the kind of external details of costume, makeup, accent, use of the body, that have always been the actor's hallmarks. Both heavily accented characterizations take enormous risks. Olivier plays Othello as a swaggering, insolent black man and Shylock as a conniving Jew. He was accused of insulting blacks and Jews, of reducing Shakespeare's majestic heroes to racial cartoons. These two roles are among his most controversial interpretations, and the wildly mixed critical receptions echo the reviews of Olivier's first major unorthodox approach to classical acting, in the 1935 John Gielgud *Romeo and Juliet*.

His unsentimental treatment of Shylock both pleased and outraged critics and audiences. On the affirmative side, John Barber, in the *Daily Telegraph*, wrote: "Unlike some Olivier performances, the studied external detail seems to proceed from the passion within. He has created a man of flint in no way admirable except for his obsessed pride of race." On the negative side, Harold Hobson, in the Sunday *Times*, commented: "Dancing with glee at Antonio's misfortunes, coming to court to cut off the pound of flesh with a briefcase more prominent than a knife, and after sentence apparently falling down stairs off-stage, Sir Laurence will not be remembered for his Shylock. Or if he is, he will be singularly unlucky."[3]

Hobson, however, applauded Olivier's equally radical concept of Othello: "Sensational it is: who would have believed that Sir Laurence could make his voice so deep and dark . . .? The power, passion and verisimilitude of Sir Laurence's performance will be spoken of with wonder for a long time to come." Jonathan Miller was not so appreciative: "What he gives us is a Notting Hill Gate Negro—a law student from Ghana—and his portrait is made up of all the ludicrous liberal cliche attitudes towards Negroes: beautiful skin, marvelous sense of rhythm, wonderful way of walking, etc. (I believe this wonderful way of walking is in fact limited to a certain type of modern show-biz Negro.) Shakespeare's Othello was a Moor, an Arab, and to emphasize his being *black* in this way makes nonsense of the play."[4]

Many American reviews repeated Jonathan Miller's objections. Critics accused Olivier of turning Othello into a vaudevillian darkie, a buffoon in blackface. Reviewers who thought Olivier looked like Al Jolson painted up to sing "Mammy" protested the racial stereotyping; and they mocked the interpretation as the great actor's great mistake. But to object to Olivier's concept of Othello as a black man is foolhardy, since the color theme is an integral part of the play: Desdemona's father is horrified because she has married a man of a different color. In deciding to play Othello the way he did, Olivier surely was violating no moral code; his interest in the role, after all, was in its opportunities for him as an actor rather than as a public speaker on race relations.

Olivier prepared for the performance like an athlete getting into shape for a major event. He trained in a gym several days a week, lifting weights, jogging, swimming, practicing breathing exercises. He lowered his natural baritone to a sepulchral bass, patterning his pitch and his vocal rhythms on West Indians he had studied in the streets and pubs of London with the shrewd eye of a mimic. The result of the meticulous preparation is that Olivier transformed himself into his idea of Othello the way he melted into his mask for Richard III. These two roles, so spectacularly different, are Olivier's most celebrated masks. For Richard, he pinched his voice into a higher, more tightened register than his own mellifluous baritone; his Richard is angular, with sharp lines both visually and aurally, whereas his Othello luxuriates in a basso profundo richness and thickness, the vowels romantically elongated, the rhythm of the sentences flowing in graceful curves. The first time we hear this Othello, we're a little jolted: the voice is so deep and august, so commanding. When Othello recounts to the senators the stories he told Desdemona of his travels, his "black magic" is apparent, for we can see how he bewitched her, in that seductive, low voice, with stories of the anthropophagi and of men whose heads grow beneath their shoulders. A proud soldier, imperial in his bearing, swelled in self-esteem, the Othello of these first scenes is a man primed for a fall. From the opening moments, this strutting, sensual man, this virile hero, fatally lacks self-awareness, and he is therefore a likely target for the clever Iago.

So clearly nonintellectual, so foolishly proud and smug, Olivier's Moor is easily duped by Frank Finlay's cold, rational villain. Iago controls the action—he is the calculating master of ceremonies—but Olivier's outsized Othello is so emotionally heroic that he takes over the play. This may well be Olivier's least yielding performance. Several critics accused him of casting the production with actors who could not compete with him, and it's true that the performance doesn't have a true ensemble unity. Olivier's acting is scaled so much higher than that of any of the other performers that he seems at times to be acting in glorious isolation, his interpretation a torrential outpouring of technical virtuosity done for its own sake.

Frank Finlay's modestly scaled Iago, more credible on film than in the theater, is subtle and intelligent, but unduly restrained since he never reveals the character's satanic undercurrents. Finlay doesn't have the authority or the insinuating, serpentine quality that a Redgrave or a Gielgud could bring to the part. Maggie Smith's Desdemona is also not entirely adjusted to the star performance. As a light comedienne, Maggie Smith is incomparably droll; but with her dry, mocking voice, her clipped rhythm and rebuking tone, she is an unromantic Desdemona. Her performance is certainly skillful, and she, like all the actors, draws power from Olivier's electric presence, but her arch characterization is more suited to Congreve than to the tumultuous world of *Othello*. She seems too witty and self-protective, too knowing, to fall for a man who woos her with tall stories and an athlete's muscled physique. Desdemona's passion, ideally, should match Othello's, but Maggie Smith's urbane character remains somewhat aloof from the Moor's extreme sensuality.

With its rudimentary visual embellishment, its proscenium aura in composition and movement, its routine use of the camera and its choppy editing, the film of *Othello* exists only as a sketchy framework for an enormous performance. There are only a few moments where film means have been used imaginatively to enhance the story or the acting. Much of the play's melodramatic narrative momentum is based on eavesdropping, and the spatial relationships between the eavesdropper and those he is spying on are effectively rendered in several deep focus compositons in which both groups of characters are framed in the same shot. Before Othello's epileptic seizure, there is a high-angle shot, as Othello falls to the ground, that enhances the climactic moment. For the most part, however, the space is cramped, cinematically unconvincing, with a painted sky indicating threatening changes in the weather. There is a wild discrepancy between the psychological truth of Olivier's acting and the patent artificiality of the decor. Olivier looks at any moment capable of dismantling the entire papier-mâché set with a single bellow. Stuart Burge's almost arrogantly indifferent direction does no more than provide a neutral frame for Olivier's fireworks.

In his other Shakespearean roles on film (even in the immature *As You Like It*), Olivier played for the camera, while here he makes no such concessions. He begins, though, as if he were about to do just that, to scale down his voltage for the greater intimacy provided by the camera. But he is only teasing, he is only setting up Othello for a fall. He comes on, swaggering, smelling a rose, his white robes a shocking contrast to his dark skin. (It is typical of the boldness of the performance that Olivier makes Othello pitch black.) Othello is humming mindlessly to himself; here is a terrifically self-pleased man, proud of his body and his social status; here is a complacent bourgeois without a care in the world. Almost throwing away his lines, Olivier plays his first scenes quietly, with a sly, delicious humor as he subtly ridicules Othello's pomposity and vanity. This low-key opening is part of a series of contrasts with which he builds his performance.

At the beginning, then, he acts with a studied detachment, commenting from above on Othello's pride and gullibility—he plays the character as being seduced by his own act. But once Iago arouses his jealousy, and Othello begins to have visions of Desdemona with Cassio; once Othello, that is, begins to lose his confidence, his belief in his invulnerable sexuality, Olivier's energy soars. He enacts sexual jealousy with primal force. There are almost literally breathtaking moments when we seem to be seeing the character hold on to reason by the slenderest of threads, and in these scenes of high, naked passion, the distinction between actor and role evaporates as we watch an elemental acting-out of rage and sorrow and sexual longing. Seemingly ignoring the camera, playing thunderously to the topmost gallery, Olivier takes enormous risks in these flights of delirious emotion. His ecstatic performance in these climactic passages is an example of a kind of grandiose classical acting unmatched in English-language films.

With Olivier's sly cooperation, the camera magnifies the actor's craft, exposing his technical cunning—his voice control, his daringly sustained pauses, his leaps in pitch and volume, his breathing. Olivier clearly exults in the chance the camera gives him to show off his skills; he's like a body-builder flexing his muscles. We are made aware of his resourcefulness, but at the same time that we admire his craft we are also swept up in his passion.

Olivier breaks almost all the rules—and wins. By any reasonable application of the requirements of film acting, this should be a ludicrous performance. It is not. It is a great one, the only example on film of tragic acting in the heroic mold. In its bravura technique and its outsized emotion, the performance is both shocking and exhilarating.

Olivier in Regional America

In his most recent venture in filmed theater, Olivier undertook management of a series of televised plays entitled *A Tribute to the American Theater*. His original plan was to produce a number of noteworthy plays for television, but the project was discontinued after the first two presentations because, according to the publicity, of Olivier's conflicting film commitments, though it is more likely, however, that the "tribute" ended because the first two offerings were so uninspired. Like most British actors, Olivier has never had a true feeling for the American idiom; his distance, in sensibility and technique, from the flavor of both Tennessee Williams's *Cat on a Hot Tin Roof* and William Inge's *Come Back, Little Sheba*, the two quintessentially American plays that opened the series in 1977, was pointedly evident. Williams's South and Inge's Midwest proved almost equally remote to him. His renditions of Big Daddy, Williams's dynamic patriarch dying of cancer, and of Doc, Inge's defeated alcoholic, count as two notable failures. Typically, Olivier selected two sharply contrasted characters to open the series, and typically, too, both performances require accents and makeup; the attempts at self-transformation don't ring true, however.

As the original Big Daddy in Elia Kazan's 1955 Broadway production (and again in the first-rate 1958 film, directed by Richard Brooks), Burl Ives was unbeatable. He had exactly the right qualities for the role: the massive physique, the blustering, cornpone conviviality. By comparison, Olivier's hardy Southern patriarch seems synthetic. Big Daddy, who carps at the mendacity of his doctors and his family, who despises his fat wife and his gutless son Gooper, and who is genuinely disappointed in his favorite son Brick and attracted to his lusty, desperate daughter-in-law Maggie, has the mocking humor, the galling irony, that are among Olivier's specialties. But Olivier can't fully release the character's rich sarcasm and earthy wisdom because he simply doesn't look or sound right in the part. Big Daddy is common stock, a vulgar, self-made tycoon. Olivier can't conceal his British decorum and his good breeding; he is too well-spoken, and too genteel, to capture Big Daddy's particular brand of bluster and gregariousness.

Whatever integrity the impersonation does have is thoroughly undermined by the choppy cutting which breaks the flow of the lines, and by the series of fake climaxes that serve as cues for commercial breaks, as well as by the remarkable ineptitude of Natalie Wood as Maggie (how one longs for the wit and vitality of Elizabeth Taylor's Maggie in the film version) and Robert Wagner as Brick. Olivier requested these two film actors to appear with him—another demonstration of his lack of feeling for the American tone. Wood is impossible; with her dead eyes and her hollow, little-girl voice, she conveys none of the sensuality or sexual desperation of one of Williams's wittiest and most agreeable female characters. Wagner succeeds only in registering Brick's sullenness, suggesting none of the character's sexual hysteria about his attraction to his dead friend Skipper or his distaste for Maggie's sexual presence. Only Maureen

Stapleton as Big Mama communicates some of the play's lusty humor.

Olivier's production of *Come Back, Little Sheba* is almost as disappointing. Olivier plays Doc, who is one of those modest, withdrawn characters to whom he has been periodically attracted as an antidote to the many heroic swaggerers he plays with such comparative ease. Inge's small-town character, a man ruined by drink, is a failure. Olivier never quite discovers the appropriate tone for him. His accent is again no more than a good try—he sounds like someone trying to pass for an American. Doc remains a passive, forlorn character for most of the play, and in these early scenes Olivier acts with a wry, wistful quality, his body slouched over a kitchen table or slumped in an easychair, his mouth slanted downward as a token of the character's defeat, his eyes by turns hollow and, when he is talking to the pretty young girl who rooms with him and his wife, filled with longing. The big opportunity comes in the last act when, taking to drink again, he goes mad, threatening to kill his wife and to tear down the house. After his crack-up, he cries for forgiveness from his wife. In these scenes, Olivier plays with full force, but these big moments don't seem to spring from the character he has been playing for three-fourths of the play. The performance isn't conceived as a whole, so that the final explosions seem more like a display of Olivier's fire and thunder than an extension of the sad character we were introduced to in the beginning of the play.

Again, as in *Cat on a Hot Tin Roof*, Olivier seems to be creating his performance in a vacuum, since Joanne Woodward as the wife is strangely remote. Woodward has played the same kind of frowsy housewife in films, so she ought to have been successful in the role. But she seems outside the part, underrehearsed and blurry, with only occasional suggestions of the character's warmth and sentimentality as she mourns her lost youth. Like Olivier in comparison to Burl Ives as Big Daddy, Woodward is overshadowed by the memory of Shirley Booth's definitive portrayal of Inge's lost, faded, small-town woman.

Olivier was attracted to both Big Daddy and Doc because he realized that neither character was comfortably within his temperamental or vocal range. His characterizations for these downhome American types are interesting patchworks and, as always when he fails, he does so honorably.

7

Character Actor

OLIVIER'S RECORD for the past twenty-five years indicates his seriousness about and commitment to films. Since the early 1950s, Olivier has regularly divided his time between films and theater; even during his period of greatest involvement with theater, when he was director of the National from 1963 to 1973, he continued to be available for film roles. And until very recently, when he has appeared in pulp like *Marathon Man* (1976) and *The Betsy* (1978), he chose challenging roles in films that were in some way significant, so that his record in films during this period is further evidence of his continual development and self-discovery as an actor, regardless of the medium.

Lured by colorful supporting roles in which he could experiment with makeup and accents, he was rarely the star, and though his name gave prestige to a project, it certainly did not insure financial success. His sequence of roles suggests interesting comparisons and cross-references, and the parts can be grouped into periods during which he was working on a particular technical problem or exploring a new kind of characterization. Sometimes, the actor plays the same kind of part in two films in a row; sometimes two roles in succession are so markedly different that they seem to have been chosen to advertise Olivier's versatility. His exuberant Macheath in *The Beggar's Opera* (1953) is a startling contrast to his low-keyed Hurstwood in *Carrie* (1951). His mundane Inspector in *Bunny Lake Is Missing* (1965) is a variation on his withdrawn schoolmaster in *Term of Trial* (1962) and his failed vaudevillian in *The Entertainer* (1960). His aristocratic Crassus in *Spartacus* (1960) has the same kind of stentorian manner, the same oratorical skill, the same larger-than-life personality, as his elegant General Burgoyne in *The Devil's Disciple* (1959). With his darkened skin and his thick accent, his Mahdi in

135

Olivier as George Hurstwood with Jennifer Jones as Carrie in William Wyler's Carrie *(1951).*

Khartoum (1966) indebted to his work in *Othello*. And his farcical
rendition of a military man in *Oh What a Lovely War!* (1969) is a
send-up of his heroic major in *The Battle of Britain* (1969). Both the
choice and the sequence of these roles are reminders of Olivier's
absorption in technique and of his objective approach to solving
problems of characterization.

Carrie

After an eleven-year absence, Olivier decided to return to Hol-
lywood when William Wyler, to whom he credits his evolution into
a good film actor, offered him the part of Hurstwood in his film of
Theodore Dreiser's *Sister Carrie*. Since it requires him to have an
American accent and to decline from gentleman of culture to a
Bowery drunk, the role was certainly tempting. At the same time,
Vivien Leigh was going to Hollywood to play Blanche du Bois in *A
Streetcar Named Desire*, and in prospect it looked as if they would
both have the same kind of popular and artistic success they had had
a dozen years earlier with *Wuthering Heights* and *Gone With the
Wind*. Leigh's performance as Tennessee Williams's magnificently
neurotic Southern belle even surpassed her Scarlett O'Hara;
Wyler's film, however, was a disappointment, and Olivier wasn't
enticed to Hollywood again for almost a decade.

With its strong narrative and its vivid period backgrounds,
Dreiser's clumsy, long-winded, and yet thoroughly compelling
novel has the ingredients for a movie blockbuster; but the film
misses Dreiser's scope and his energy. The novel traces a country
girl's contamination by the forces of the big city. Although Chicago
and New York are powerful presences in the book, on film the cities
don't have the same force. Even more crucial, though, is the way
the film softens Carrie's character. Dreiser's rustic heroine is an
opportunist who would rather be a kept woman than an underpaid
factory worker. She is motivated by economic self-interest, and
when the men she entices cease to be of use to her, she leaves them.
When the novel was published, in 1900, many readers were
shocked at the way Dreiser treats his heroine, for, though she has
offended conventional morality, she is not punished in a conventional way. Unlike similar characters in numerous Victorian novels,
Carrie does not end up poor or downtrodden or forsaken. Instead,
she has become a famous actress who has made her way into the
wealthy inner city that the younger, dewy-eyed Carrie yearned for.

She is unhappy, as it is her fate always to want more than she has, but she has survived and prospered in a harsh environment. Since he seemed to regard his clearly erring heroine with what, at the time, was an unsettling neutrality, Dreiser smashed stodgy Victorian notions; and his descriptions of the glitter and lure of money are so vivid that at times he even seemed to share Carrie's lust for wealth and the Finer Things.

Caught up in the city's rush, Carrie is a passive heroine who collects men and establishes a career almost by chance, and rather than condemning her, Dreiser suggests that she was smart enough to embrace opportunity. If Carrie, finally, isn't an endearing heroine, she isn't contemptible, either, and we can't help admiring her determination even as we notice that the innocent and charming country girl whom we first meet has hardened into a knowing woman of the world.

Though the film's heroine goes through the same experiences as Dreiser's, she never really loses her innocence. The film is reluctant to disturb our first impression of Carrie as a naive charmer, and it therefore contains only fleeting glimpses of her as either sour or hardened. Because her motivations are blurred, it is never clear exactly how we are supposed to be responding to her. Jennifer Jones plays Carrie charmingly, stressing the character's freshness and sentimentality; but in the later scenes, when her marriage to Hurstwood deteriorates and when she leaves him a broken man in order to pursue her stage career, her movie-heroine smiles and her flouncy manner deny the true thrust of the material.

Olivier's character doesn't violate the moral norm, and so Hurstwood is safer to dramatize than Carrie is. Hurstwood is a conventional figure from Victorian melodrama who is heavily punished for his crimes of bigamy and theft since he ends up a shattered old man in a Bowery flophouse. The character is less complex than Carrie, and he isn't as essential to Dreiser's theme; Wyler decided to focus on him precisely because he did not offend Hollywood morality.

Olivier is careful not to play Hurstwood as the villain in a temperance melodrama. He avoids an obvious, tearjerking interpretation of this urbane man who loses his grasp on his world; from the opening, when we first see Hurstwood socializing with the prosperous clientele in the elegant restaurant he manages, Olivier is downbeat and subtle. As he walks through the restaurant, wearing a mask of affa-

bility, he suggests the distracted air of a man who is riddled with
dissatisfaction; he's a volcano of repressed anxieties. Without
straining, Olivier turns Dreiser's victim into a complex modern
neurotic. Since his character seems doomed from the start, he glides
effortlessly into the final passages that depict the character's decline.
Bypassing easy pathos and rampages, Olivier avoids all the
stereotyped ways of playing a drunk; as Hurstwood retreats into
himself, the actor's movements and speech become heavier and

Olivier as the highwayman, Macheath, in John Gay's *The Beggar's Opera* (1953).

more methodical, though even in despair he retains his dignity. Although Olivier's American accent is imperfect, the hints of English pronunciation underscore the character's patrician manner and help to give him an appropriate aura of pretentiousness.

Olivier's performance is often cited as one of his few mistakes, when in fact it is thoroughly original. He takes the chance of playing against audience sympathy by making Hurstwood aloof and private, and instead of playing a drunk like a big star actor lusting after an Oscar, he is content to create a small, subtle picture of a deeply repressed and self-destructive man.

The Beggar's Opera

Olivier's Macheath, in *The Beggar's Opera*, made in England the following year, is a complete reversal of his understatement in Wyler's film. Olivier selected the part in this picture in order to correct his image as a staid classical actor, and he patterns John Gay's famous highwayman on the swashbuckling heroics of Douglas Fairbanks. He sings (in a light, pleasant baritone); he dances; he woos many women; he climbs up and down ladders and haylofts; he rides a horse—he carries on, in short, as if he were the leading man in a Saturday-afternoon action special. Olivier had earned praise for the athleticism of some of his stage performances, but he hadn't had much opportunity on film to demonstrate his gymnastic skills.

He plays Macheath for superficial qualities; he's handsome, lithe, sensual, and he erases the aloofness that is often a part of his characterizations. Olivier works hard to sustain the gusto of Gay's roguish hero; but even here he varies mood and tempo. In the scenes with Jenny Diver and the whores, he's priapic; in the courtship scenes with Lucy and Polly, he's gentle and sly. With his fellow highwaymen, he acts like a dapper businessman, and in the gaming parlor, he is an elegant man about town. In order not to mar the consistent high spirits of Gay's ballad opera, Olivier keeps it all light and sketchy.

Peter Brook's uncertain direction, however, undermines Olivier's ebullience. Brook is eager to let us know right from the start that he has turned Gay's play into a film, and so our first view of Macheath is on the open range, galloping jauntily through a vernal landscape. Since Gay's opera is set in the narrow, crowded streets, the steaming brothels, and the dank prison of the city's underworld, Brook's hearty, open-air introduction altogether violates the material's Hogarthian vision of the city.

Once Brook goes indoors, however, he begins to discover Gay's pagan carnival spirit, and the film finds a style that embellishes the play. Brook, though, was clearly a novice at the time (this was his first film), and he only hints at the kind of dark, radical vision that marked his stage productions of *Marat/Sade* and *King Lear*. This *Beggar's Opera* often looks too bright and clean, when what it really needs is the pestilential atmosphere that served *Marat/Sade* so memorably. Further, Brook's frenetic camera movement and fractured editing—he did not want to be accused of staginess—are needlessly overexcited.

Christopher Fry's adaptation removes most of Gay's topical references to political figures and his mockery of opera and opera divas of the day; and it minimizes Gay's satire of highwaymen trying to imitate the manners of the gentry. Fry has provided a new frame for Macheath's story—the opera is performed by prison inmates. The sinister prison setting, and the final scenes in which the prisoners engage in a bacchanalian dance that breaks down the separation between actor and role, surely influenced Brook's direction of *Marat/Sade*. Because it must be understood against its theatrical and historical context as an ironic inversion of the anemic sentimental comedy popular in the early eighteenth century, *The Beggar's Opera* (written in 1728) is a difficult work for contemporary audiences, though its vibrant score and its satiric attacks on greed and lust and selfishness have continued to delight theatergoers. The film does not have the swinging, lusty quality of the original, but neither does it look like filmed theater, and it provides a pleasing adornment to Olivier's film career.

The Devil's Disciple *and* Spartacus

In both *The Devil's Disciple* and *Spartacus*, Olivier's lordly English tone is used as a contrast to Kirk Douglas's muscular, plain-spoken American manner. The difference between the English and American style is in fact one of Shaw's central themes in *The Devil's Disciple*; in *Spartacus*, Olivier's diction and bearing depict the effete manner of a Roman aristocrat, whereas Douglas's straightforward, homespun quality underlines the democratic spirit of the rebel slave. In both films, Olivier's reserve and elegance are offset by Douglas's burly directness; Olivier is thus the foil to Douglas's adventurous heroes and, more than in most of his film work, Olivier performs with the aura of an eminent stage actor.

General Burgoyne, an imperious gentleman who speaks almost exclusively in epigrams and quips, is one of Shaw's most delightful characters. "Without a conquest, you cannot have an aristocracy," he announces loftily. "History will tell lies, as usual," he predicts. "Have you any idea of the average marksmanship of the army of His Majesty King George the Third?" he inquires of the renegade hero. "If we make you up a firing party, what will happen? Half of them will miss you: the rest will make a mess of the business and leave you to the provo-Marshal's pistol. Whereas we can hang you in a perfectly workmanlike and agreeable way. Let me persuade you to be hanged, Mr. Anderson?" he asks urbanely, as if he were inquiring of a guest if he preferred one or two lumps of sugar in his tea.

General Burgoyne is clearly Shaw's spokesman, for he has the wit, the clear-headedness, the dispassionate posture, of the playwright himself. Shaw was enchanted with him; and in his afterword to the play, he adds to his portrait by offering information (at great length) about the historical General. Olivier gives Burgoyne a trim cutting edge, making every crackling line seem like a brisk riposte or a jibe. He tosses off the character's sly inversions and bons mots with a teasing glint in his eye, playing the patronizing General as though he were a worldly, caustic Restoration gallant. Burgoyne is a small, superficial character part that relies on Olivier's imperial bearing and remoteness; it is one of the few times in films when he exploits a stereotyped notion of how an illustrious British stage actor is supposed to "behave." Yet his immaculate performance is irresistible.

In Shaw's play, the General comes on only in Act III, but happily he is sprinkled throughout the film. In allowing him a fuller participation in the action, the scriptwriters actually improved on Shaw. *The Devil's Disciple* is usually classed along with Hollywood's other failed attempts to capture the Shavian spirit, and when it was released in 1959, only Olivier was spared from the critics' displeasure. But the film intelligently rearranges Shaw's rigid three-act structure, and it includes action scenes that amplify the Revolutionary War background without disturbing Shaw's thesis. Despite the Hollywood trimmings—the battle scenes, the big stars—the film remains a drama of ideas on the Shavian theme of character reversal. As in the play, Dick Dudgeon, the devil's disciple, and Reverend Anderson exchange roles, the latter discovering that he is a man of action and the renegade learning that he in fact is a true Christian.

As Shaw's common-sensical hero who demolishes Puritan hy-
pocrisy and romantic sentimentality, Kirk Douglas has exactly the
right kind of energy and directness; and Burt Lancaster's Reverend
Anderson is clearly a swashbuckling hero in uncomfortable disguise.

Douglas and Lancaster are vigorous American types whose personalities and acting style offer a decided contrast to Olivier; and in
insisting on the difference between the American movie actors and
the celebrated English man of the theater, the film highlights the
play's dialectic in a thoroughly agreeable way.

One of the most powerful sequences in *Spartacus* establishes a
parallel between Olivier's lofty oration to his soldiers and Kirk
Douglas's blunt speech to his warrior slaves. The cross-cutting between the speeches enforces the difference between the patrician
and the populist style. Olivier's rhetorical manner is cunning, formidable; Douglas is democratic and earthy. Olivier's Crassus speaks
for imperialist ideals: "I promise you a new Rome, a new Italy, a
new Empire, the restoration of order." Spartacus is the communist
savior: "As long as we live, we must stay true to ourselves. I do know
that we're brothers and that we're free." Crassus stands apart from
his soldiers, on the marble steps of the Capitol; Spartacus remains
close to his listeners, who sit on the ground before him and look up
as though he were delivering the Sermon on the Mount. High-angle
shots of the slaves looking up at their leader reinforce their awe of
Spartacus; low-angle shots of Crassus on the steps emphasize his
tyranny.

In *The Devil's Disciple*, Olivier's elegance has wit and charm,
whereas in *Spartacus* it is a token of villainy. Dalton Trumbo, in the
first screenplay for which he received credit after having been
blacklisted during the 1950s witch hunt, is transfixed by the difference between the corrupt aristocrat and the saintly slave, between
the slick, manipulative politician and the rough, selfless leader of
the people. In this sweeping communist epic, Olivier is on the
wrong side of the class struggle—he plays the kind of character who
dispossessed Trumbo.

For his role as an evil Roman, Olivier's face becomes a mask of
decadence. He is forbiddingly cold and disdainful. In his first scene,
as he and other dissipated aristocrats select gladiators as if they were
ordering items on a menu, he is chillingly remote and magisterial.
In the Senate, as he argues for the restoration of the old order, and

on the steps of the Capitol, as he exhorts his soldiers, he is a skillful orator capable, like Shakespeare's Mark Antony, of virtuoso manipulations of public opinion. Cool, authoritative, *masked*, Olivier's Crassus is a vivid portrait of political cynicism. But Trumbo's intelligent script reveals the insecure neurotic that crouches beneath the controlling public figure. Crassus confuses his lust for political power with sexual conquest: "I shall not violate Rome at the moment of possessing her." "There is only one way to deal with Rome," he whispers to a handsome slave he is obliquely trying to seduce, "you must serve her, abase yourself before her, you must grovel at her feet. You must . . . [delicious Olivier pause here] love her." Though the script contains the preposterous implication that Crassus's preference for men is somehow linked to his obsessive drive to power, Olivier's seductions of a houseboy (Tony Curtis) and of a youthful Julius Caesar (John Gavin) are among the most bizarre love scenes in films, his aspirate voice silky and insinuating, his eyes beckoning beneath the steel.

Crassus's confrontation with Spartacus also has sexual undertones. He is jealous and afraid of his political enemy, and he wants to seduce the rebel slave's wife (Jean Simmons). "Why do you love Spartacus?" he demands of her, a look of panic in his eyes. "Your wife and your child are slaves in my household," he taunts Spartacus in their final encounter. Because Spartacus doesn't respond the way Crassus wants him to, the tyrant screams at the tied slave, beating him with his fists. Olivier turns the film's villain into a twisted, wounded animal grasping for self-respect. Masterfully, he makes Crassus a driven, complicated character, a misfit, a grotesque; and a huge costume drama becomes in part a serious examination of a political madman.

Olivier's immense performance, which gives Crassus more shading than Trumbo had intended, and which has the stature of great classical acting, is a fitting ornament to one of Hollywood's most literate spectacles. *Spartacus* is one of the great epic films, comparable in its handling of crowds and battles to the work of D. W. Griffith and Eisenstein. Stanley Kubrick's direction, with its lengthy tracking shots and deep-focus compositions, enhances Trumbo's sharply pointed script; this is a big-budget Hollywood film that has a truly enlightened political point of view. Olivier was very unhappy working on it, but Kubrick's underrated film has the magnitude and visual elegance of a genuine epic.

The Entertainer and Term of Trial

Olivier's performances in *The Devil's Disciple* and *Spartacus* are striking, but the actor didn't want to be limited to playing larger-than-life historical characters and he didn't want to be typed as a classical performer out of touch with modern trends. So in the late 1950s, at the time of a resurgence in English drama, and when he felt he was in danger of becoming "dangerously more staid," he wanted very much to test himself in contemporary roles. He went to the Royal Court Theatre to appear in two modern plays, John Osborne's *The Entertainer* and Ionesco's *Rhinoceros*. For the leading classical actor to appear at the Court in experimental plays was exactly the kind of risk that Olivier always savored.

In 1956, Osborne's *Look Back in Anger* had opened at the Court, and critics treated the event as the beginning of a new era in English drama. The play gave to the theater a new type, the Angry Young Man, in the character of Jimmy Porter, who rages against the system without doing anything to change it. Jimmy was a modern antihero, a rebel without a program. Though he was not an admirable character, he had negative energy, and he seemed to speak for the assorted dissatisfactions of a generation. He became a symptomatic hero, a representative of modern malaise, and Osborne's play became a landmark in modern theater history. *Look Back in Anger* introduced what seemed at the time like a new realism into the theater; the play's working-class milieu, and its bitter hero, were a direct challenge to the drawing-room settings and the well-bred characters that had traditionally dominated the British popular theater. Here was a character who, despite his remarkable articulateness, presumably talked the language of the common man; here was rude proletarian drama that smashed the decorum of the well-made play.

Look Back in Anger inaugurated a cycle of dramas about the working class. In the late 1950s and early 1960s, social realist plays and films dominated British entertainment: films like *Look Back in Anger, Saturday Night and Sunday Morning, A Kind of Loving, A Taste of Honey,* and *Loneliness of the Long Distance Runner* gave British movies a new international identity. The movement of social realism, called Free Cinema, and incorporating the settings and character types associated with the theatrical "kitchen sink" realism of Osborne's trend-setting play, was technically showier than most English films had been before this. Directors like Tony Richardson,

Lindsay Anderson, and Richard Lester used film technique in more
knowing and self-conscious ways than the typically sedate English
film before this period. Photographed on location, the dramas would
often be punctuated with hectic editing, a mobile hand-held camera, extreme angles. Like the contemporary French New Wave, the
English Free Cinema mixed formative and realist methods and indicated an infatuation with film language: these films were made by
directors who loved movies.

In the late 1950s, then, there was a sense in British theater and
films of expansion and exploration, in both subject matter and
technique, and Olivier wanted to become a part of the new tenden-
cies. He therefore went to the Court to appear in *The Entertainer*, a
new play by Osborne, the catalyst of the new realism, and he also
worked in films like *Term of Trial* (1962) that were examples of the
"modernist" experiments.

In taking on the roles of the entertainer in Osborne's play, of
Berenger in *Rhinoceros*, of the provincial schoolteacher in *Term of
Trial*, and of the antihero in a West End comedy of provincial manners called *Semi-Detached*, Olivier meant to declare his sympathy
with the modern note and to step down for a while from the
exalted heights of classical tragedy. In these contemporary dramas
and films, he played varieties of the common man—failures, average
guys, obscure small-town fellows, characters antithetical in temperament and rank to the proud kings that had secured his reputation. Except for his performance as Archie Rice, the entertainer, an
impersonation that is commonly regarded as his greatest outside the
classics, Olivier was not especially well received in these departures
from his usual milieu. Kenneth Tynan suggests that Olivier "seldom
succeeds" in these roles (undertaken, Tynan feels, "out of a sense of
duty") because his "outsized emotional candor cannot help breaking
through, the actor impatiently bursts the seams of the role, and the
common man becomes extraordinary."[1]

In *Semi-Detached* (1962), Olivier played a small-time operator
whose lust for bourgeois respectability was concealed beneath a
manner of devastating averageness. The play wasn't a success, and
Olivier wasn't well reviewed—critics wondered why the preeminent classical actor should be detained by a farce set in the pro-
vinces—but his choice was shrewd, for David Turner's cleverly constructed, Molièresque satire in modern dress enabled him to
explore a new kind of comic style. Tynan told him that *Semi-Detached* failed because "it's extremely cruel and you are making the

audience suffer, and that's the idea of the play; you can't always do that and get away with it. . . . It was the first time you'd played a complete swine without any redeeming charm or pathos."[2]

Olivier's comparative failure with unheroic characters was reversed when he played Archie Rice. Along with his Richard III, Oedipus, and Edgar in *The Dance of Death*, his Archie is a performance that other actors recall with particular respect. As Richard Findlater has written about Olivier's entertainer, "This masterly performance was acting *about* acting, its shams and realities; it was the personification of a dying theatre and (less certainly) a dying society; but it was also the incarnation of one man's suffering and despair, nonetheless overwhelming in its theatrical truth because the man was a third-rate comic rather than a Shakespearean king."[3]

Olivier also played Archie Rice in the film version of *The Entertainer*, and Tony Richardson (who had also directed the play) opened up the material by giving it the look of "kitchen-sink" realism of other films of the period. The seaside setting is used for its seediness and out-of-season isolation, and the film has the grim, stark quality that signaled integrity in the English social realist dramas in the late 1950s and early 1960s.

The forlorn characters dribble their lives away in dingy boarding-houses overrun with hideous flowered wallpaper and in crowded, rundown pubs. There is no sun in these British films noirs, and little joy: these characters are a sorry group who represent the decline of England.

The Entertainer is a conventional example of the new realism distinguished by Olivier's searing impersonation of the failed entertainer. In the play, Osborne surrounds and punctuates the naturalistic domestic story with examples of Archie's vaudeville routines. In these framing vignettes, Olivier established direct contact with the audience, as he had on film as Richard III. For the film of *The Entertainer*, the vaudeville interludes do not noticeably depart, in visual style or performance technique, from the realism of the central story about Archie's family relationships—his teasing, respectful attitude to his father, also a vaudevillian and a good one; his mixture of irritation with and compassion for the frowsy wife he constantly betrays by seducing other women; his shyness with his intellectual, politically involved daughter, who acts and feels like a stranger whenever she comes to visit.

Archie Rice is one of Olivier's most compelling masks. In one of his dazzling transformations, Olivier plays a performer of no talent whatsoever. His renditions of Archie's music-hall turns are macabre charades that expose the character's hollowness, terror, and self-contempt. Archie's inane comic patter, his cracked singing voice, his mannequinlike movements, his blank eyes, are naked revelations of character; Olivier gives Archie's performances a grisly, sinister quality—there is something frightening and finally pathetic in this man's self-exposure before an audience. Submerging himself beneath the character's pained, grinning mask, Olivier erases his own mannerisms, and we respond to Archie's failure rather than to Olivier's brilliance.

To enact Osborne's burnt-out case, Olivier deadens his eyes, slurs his crisp diction, slackens his body. He looks and sounds like a man gone to seed. The character is similar to others that Olivier has played in that he is caustic, patronizing, an actor both onstage and off; but Olivier blurs the haughty, authoritative quality that identified many of his earlier performances in ironic parts. Archie is softer, more vulnerable, than most of the characters he has played. As Archie tells jokes to entertain his family, as he tries too strenu-

Olivier as Archie Rice in *The Entertainer* (1960).

ously to be the life of the party both at work and at home, Olivier lets us see the character's desperation and loneliness. In one scene, after he's tried to be jolly, he turns to his daughter, his convivial manner dropped, his shoulders sagging, his eyes pleading, and whispers urgently, "Talk to me." It is a heartbreaking moment. Another startling moment is the moan of pain when he hears that his son, a soldier, has been killed. Olivier is too honest to milk the part for easy pathos; by emphasizing his bitterness, his selfishness, his callous treatment of his wife, his condescension to his father, and his remoteness from his children, he makes it difficult to like the character. Olivier enlarges the material, and if *The Entertainer* is not finally the elegy for a dying civilization that Osborne intended, it is at least a haunting study of failure.

As a kind of companion piece to Archie Rice, Olivier chose to play a withdrawn schoolmaster in *Term of Trial,* a film with an even more somber atmosphere than that of *The Entertainer.* Another drama of provincial frustration, set in overdecorated, overheated rooms that reflect the characters' despair, *Term of Trial* looks almost like a parody of the "kitchen-sink" tradition. Olivier is studiously subdued, while Simone Signoret, playing his forlorn wife, is more successful in absorbing the ordinariness of her character. Dressed in plain, baggy sweaters and overweight, she blends perfectly into the colorless decor as she quietly brews tea or sits passively in a dumpy chair.

Olivier's impersonation of a repressed backwater teacher is not entirely convincing; the role doesn't contain the bravura opportunities of Archie Rice, and having less to work with, Olivier seems uncomfortable. Despite his efforts to scale himself down, to cloak his musical voice with an assumed tonelessness, he is still too imposing. In his first scene, however, he is unnoticeable among a group of drab-looking teachers. "I'm a very ordinary person," he says to a student (Sarah Miles) who has fallen in love with him. "I'm shopworn, more than a little afraid of life. I'm not worthy of your love." "You're so refined, you've got charm," the student insists. "You're deep, like a character in a Victorian novel, sad and romantic."

As in *Carrie,* Olivier tries to suggest a deeper characterization than the script provides. He plays the teacher as wistful and private, as secretly troubled; and he makes him wise enough to support the student's adulation. Playing against his own natural energy, he has to work to get the character's serene detachment, his gentleness and sweetness. In the scenes with Simone Signoret, he is, uncharacteristically, a silent victim: "Stop being so bloody noble about everything," his wife taunts him while he listens, head lowered in shame, his torso slumped in defeat. "I'd rather be treated badly by a man with some spirit than to put up with your mush."

Only near the end, when he finally defends himself on trial against his student's accusation of attempted rape, does the character's mask of composure crack. Having held himself back throughout the film, Olivier now opens up in the trial scene with an impassioned outburst that betrays his subdued interpretation. Delivering his defense in the grand Olivier manner, he is far too assertive and accomplished. Until this explosion, though, his performance has been very cautiously built on the assumption that less is more.

Olivier by nature is clearly not a victim, and his provincial schoolmaster looks, finally, like the experiment of a vigorous actor trying to adjust himself to the scale of a resolutely unheroic character. Three years later, in *Bunny Lake Is Missing*, he was to play another nondescript type. Before this, however, he was to undertake another major project in theater management.

8

The Later Years

Olivier at the National Theatre

WHEN HE HAD BEEN DISMISSED from management of the Old Vic in 1948, Olivier was outraged because he felt he had not been guilty of the charges leveled against him. He did not think that he had used the stage of the Old Vic for selfish star turns nor did he believe that he had been distracted by other commitments from devoting his primary attention to the company. He had, after all, played the small roles of Hotspur, Shallow, and the Button Moulder (in Ibsen's *Peer Gynt*) during the same season in which he played Oedipus. And he felt that the long and arduous tour to the Antipodes in 1948 was proof of his commitment to the company as well as of his resistance to the glamour and money offered by the West End and Hollywood.

His direction of the National Theatre, from 1963 to 1973, elicited the same kinds of criticism. He was accused of using the theater as a showcase for himself and of remaining aloof from the ensemble. In fact, however, he appeared in only a modest number of productions during his ten-year management, in some of them in distinctly supporting roles; and, furthermore, wasn't the leading actor of the English-speaking theater entitled to use the stage of the National for displays of his art? Wouldn't theatergoers have felt cheated if Olivier had confined himself merely to being a member of the ensemble? Such selflessness, of course, was not part of his temperament; by nature and talent, Olivier is a star rather than an ensemble actor, and on those occasions when he did appear at the National in a leading role he necessarily took center stage. When he played Othello in 1964, he knew and everybody else knew that audiences came to see him as Othello rather than to see a production of *Othello*

151

Olivier as the Mahdi in Khartoum *(1966).*

at the National Theatre. But he was criticized for aggravating the show-business aura of the event by not casting an actor equal to his own stature in the role of Iago. He chose Frank Finlay, a hard-working young man with limited experience in Shakespeare. Finlay could not, of course, hold the stage with Olivier, and the production became more or less a spectacular one-man show. The one time at the National that Olivier shared the stage with an actor of his own fiber was when he played with Michael Redgrave in *Uncle Vanya.*

In addition to his alleged violations of the ensemble ideal, Olivier was attacked for his choice of plays as well. Surprisingly, considering the critic's ungallant reviews of Vivien Leigh, Olivier selected Kenneth Tynan to be his literary director. Olivier often has had a fear of being thought old-fashioned, and so he allowed himself to be swayed by Tynan's often-trendy tastes. (Tynan devised *Oh, Calcutta!*) With Tynan's provocations, the staid National was more hospitable to the hip and the modern than many theatergoers felt was appropriate; there were more incursions of the avant-garde, more tamperings with and updating of classics, than the usual fare at the Old Vic had traditionally included.

Before he assumed his duties at the National, Olivier had been appointed director of the Chichester Theatre Festival. The assignment, he knew, was something of a tryout for his managerial skills. He opened his first season at the Chichester with two obscure Jacobean dramas, John Fletcher's *The Chances* and John Ford's *The Broken Heart,* both of which he directed. Tynan, always poised to attack as well as to praise Olivier, criticized him in an open letter for his misguided literary judgments. Like all theatrical managers, Olivier was being evaluated according to his ability to produce hits. In this context, he saved the season at the Chichester, and secured for himself the management of the National, by producing a palpable hit, an all-star *Uncle Vanya,* performed (as Chekhov must be) with true repertory-company cooperation. The production was received with enormous enthusiasm, as if the press wanted to insure Olivier's election to the National, and it became part of his first season as manager of Britain's premier theater.

Olivier's tenure at the National was a difficult period. He was under attack from the critics, the public, and from his coworkers. Yet few would deny his right to be in the position. It was expected that he would lead the company into its permanent home on the South Bank, but after ten years, Olivier felt the need to pass on the directorship to a younger management. (As a memorial to his management, as well as to his career as a whole, one of the three theaters that comprise the National Theatre complex is called the Olivier.) He had spent ten years as an administrator while at the same time continuing to act in films and on stage. He had certainly earned time off, though taking it easy has never been his style.

On balance, he had been a good administrator, insofar as attending to the daily business of running a theater was concerned. As public-relations representative for the National, he played his part supremely well. In statements to the press and at official gatherings, he seemed the model bureaucrat, purposeful, subdued, commonsensical. Dressed in conservative suits, his hair gray at the temples, carrying an attaché case and the ubiquitous furled umbrella, he even began to look like a city businessman. There was no trace in his bearing or appearance of the famous, temperamental actor. As always, Olivier played his part with great technical resourcefulness, assuming to perfection the external details of his "character."

Bunny Lake Is Missing and Khartoum

While he was overseeing the National Theatre, Olivier appeared in films from time to time, most memorably in *Bunny Lake is Missing* (1965) and *Khartoum* (1966). With characteristic perversity, Preminger cast Olivier in the secondary role of an imperturbable inspector, the kind of part that Jack Hawkins or John Williams could walk through. Critics complained of the scandalous waste—Olivier as a humdrum inspector!—but this is probably the actor's most successful attempt at portraying a completely unexceptional character. He doesn't try to discover more than the script gives him or to transform a stock character into a stunning star part. As the representative of the normal, workaday world, he gives the film a steady support, and his orderly inspector defines by contrast the unstable and possibly sinister world of the American brother and sister who may or may not have lost a child named Bunny Lake. Olivier's inspector is our moral anchor, and it is through him that we gauge the other characters. Because he likes the distraught American mother (Carol Lynley), we begin to appreciate and trust her, too; and his suspicion of her shifty-eyed brother (Keir Dullea) triggers our own.

In the purposeful manner of the professional sleuth, Olivier asks the questions, nodding, grimacing, smiling, while the witnesses act

their character parts with evident glee. There is a delightful encounter between Olivier and Noel Coward, who plays a wildly eccentric and decadent landlord. Coward overacts outrageously in his
finest rococo manner as Olivier stands there in deadpan disapproval.

Once he enters the case of the disappeared Bunny Lake, he functions as an unruffled, occasionally sarcastic master of ceremonies.
Commenting on human follies and on the characters' oddities, the
inspector has a mordant sense of humor. At the end, after the hunt
for the missing child, he offers his benediction to both mother and
daughter: "Go home, and get a good night's rest, now that you both
exist."

Bunny Lake Is Missing contains Olivier's most effortless, and
perhaps most unselfish, film acting. And his beautifully crafted little
performance enhances and strengthens the work of all the other
actors.

As if in accord with a grand master plan, Olivier followed the
Preminger thriller with his flamboyant performances in *Othello* and
Khartoum. For both parts, he darkens his skin, paints his lips,
lowers his voice. His Mahdi in *Khartoum,* in fact, looked like a
replay of *Othello* for those who missed the limited screenings.

Designed as showcases for Olivier, the human chameleon, both
performances are studied, mannered, gaudily theatrical: here, in
spectacular array, is the consummate actor's actor, the character
actor par excellence. The subtle, downplayed, absolutely realistic
Olivier of the Preminger film and the extroverted Olivier of *Othello*
and *Khartoum* offer sharply contrasted images, yet the actor's approach is the same. In both kinds of performance he buries himself
behind the image he creates for his characters.

The Mahdi is thus a pop rendition of the Moor transported to the
larger canvas of a Hollywood epic. Olivier uses almost the same
accent as he did for Othello, and with his deeply darkened skin and
his turban, he looks almost the same, too. The Mahdi is one of
Olivier's compulsive tyrant figures, a visionary who wants to lead an
Arab Empire and who touts himself as Mohammad's earthly representative. "I am the Expected One," he intones in a thrusting,
singsong voice. Other characters refer to him as a special being, "a
man of vision to challenge the world"; "the most extraordinary man
the Sudan has ever seen." The Mahdi wants the world to tremble at
his power. Olivier gives this self-appointed Messiah a streak of lu-
nacy, playing him with a glint in his eye that suggests a touch of the

charlatan. As in *Spartacus*, Olivier is absolutely convincing as a vigorous politician; he plays the Mahdi with such authority that the character's extravagant boasts do not seem far-fetched. Whether addressing his people or confronting his adversary Lord Douglas (Charlton Heston), the leader is always performing. This is one of Olivier's "public" performances in which we never get a glimpse of the character in a private moment.

The confrontations between Olivier's mystic warrior chieftain and Heston's rationalistic soldier are the film's strongest scenes. As he almost always does, Olivier energizes the actor he plays opposite, for Heston is more expressive in his encounters with Olivier than he is elsewhere in the film. The meetings between the two leaders have tension and edge, but the producers were clearly afraid of restricting their canvas to the political and personal conflict between the two men and they embellish the film with action and scenery that befit the Cinerama presentation. If this had been a claustrophobic, two-character Olivier film like *Sleuth*, it might have been a fascinating study of the uses of power. As it is, the conflict between the Mahdi and Gordon—between romanticism and rationality, between East and West—is an adornment to a handsome but superficial historical spectacle.

Sleuth and *Love Among the Ruins*

Sleuth (in 1972) marked Olivier's return to a big role, after a series of cameo appearances; as Pauline Kael wrote, it was "exhilarating" to see him in a big part after a succession of tantalizing bits and pieces. Anthony Shaffer's melodrama is a skillful, trifling thriller in which two characters match their wits in a brutal kind of game-playing. A famed writer of mysteries invites his wife's lover to his country estate and proceeds to entice him with a robbery scheme that is merely a set-up for humiliation. In Act II, the lover retaliates with two clever masquerades of his own.

Like many of Olivier's characters, the writer loves to act. He is a ham, and in playing him Olivier gives free rein to the streak of hamminess that was frequently a part of his liveliest performances. Shaffer's silly play releases an almost childlike exuberance in Olivier—his high-energy delivery is open testimony to his joy in acting. The characterization is filled with sly comic turns: the writer, a slightly dotty old boy, talks to himself in a variety of farcical accents (broad Americanese, English old lady) and has a complete battery of fussy mannerisms. Like the actor himself, the character is a master of disguise, a wizard of dramatic invention.

When he is in control of the game, overwhelming his victim, hopping for joy at his own ingenuity, savoring the character's lacerating wit, Olivier is irresistible. It doesn't matter that his acting is probably too busy and too boisterous because his energy—his delight in putting on a show—is really all the material has to go on.

In the second half, when his adversary gains control and the writer becomes the supplicant, Olivier's pronounced "acting" is less beguiling. Olivier is not entirely believable as a whimpering victim outsmarted by a glib hairdresser. He has been so persuasive as a man in control that he works against the script's final revelation of the character as a pathetic, impotent old man. Olivier is so vigorous and resourceful that we wonder why his character should even care if his wife wants to leave him.

Joseph L. Mankiewicz's direction appropriately emphasizes the story's theatricality and artifice. The film begins and ends with miniature stage settings, and the writer's collection of dolls, which is palpably present as a kind of chorus to the action, underlines the characters' elaborate play-acting. *Sleuth* is a duet for two skillful actors who play two skillful actors. Undaunted by the honor of playing opposite Olivier, Michael Caine charges into his role with gusto, but he does not finally persuade us that he can beat the Master in a ruthless game of deception.

Love Among the Ruins (presented on television in 1975) is also a two-character drama, one clearly designed as a vehicle for two elder statesmen. Olivier is a crusty barrister who defends a renowned actress (Katharine Hepburn) in a breach-of-contract suit from a sleek lower-class fortune hunter. The creaky story turns on the fact that the lawyer and his client met briefly forty years ago; the lawyer has idealized her as the symbol of romance while she claims that she has forgotten him. The two are clever masqueraders, instinctive fakers. Got up in an inappropriate red dress, she puts on a charade as a vain, silly woman when in fact she is thoroughly level-headed; he is an expert actor in the courtroom. Both characters play for each other as well as for the jury.

James Costigan's script, with its sly inversions and reversals, its teasing stabs at different levels of illusion, has the appearance of wit—it banks on outward show as much as the characters do. But for all its display of literacy, the dialogue misses the style of the true high comedy of Coward or Wilde to which it aspires; and the artificial script simply provides the occasion for two grand performers to entertain us.

Hepburn and Olivier recall Monroe and Olivier, as once again the technique of a star and that of a genuine actor are sharply contrasted. Erupting in her late florid manner, Hepburn is all broad gesture and declamation as she offers a strident resume of her celebrated (and maddening) mannerisms. Echoing her past work, she plays up to what her audience expects of her; she exploits their fondness for her. The absolute familiarity of what she does here is perhaps emphasized by the fact that this was the ninth film in which she was directed by George Cukor. She has charm and vitality, of course, but she is playing Katharine Hepburn rather than Costigan's character.

Because audiences (and especially American audiences) can't bring to Olivier's work the same kind of memories and associations; because he isn't the national institution that Hepburn is, he melts more easily into his role, promoting his character rather than himself. With its deft changes in rhythm, volume, and pitch, Olivier's trilling, stentorian speech to the jury is a miniature poetics of timing and intonation. But until this climactic summation, his foolishly romantic lawyer is beautifully modulated. Olivier's drawing-room manner is immensely assured; he doesn't threaten to dismantle the fragile material as he does in *Sleuth*, and he doesn't ignore the camera as in his daring overacting in *Othello* and *The Dance of Death*. His delicate performance demonstrates his absolute mastery of the technique of film acting, but he is really absurdly overqualified for Costigan's soufflé. After more than half a century devoted to perfecting his craft, Olivier deserves richer material than this.

Marathon Man and The Betsy

Unfortunately, he has only been offered worse. But he has continued to work because, as always, he thrives on the challenges offered by new roles—acting for him is a requirement, an absolute necessity—and because, as the aging father of three young children (by his third wife, Joan Plowright), he needs the money. The recent Hollywood offers to do films like *Marathon Man* (1976) and *The Betsy* (1978) have been financially very appealing to him.

"I have a large family to support and, to be perfectly frank, I always needed extra money," he said in an interview with the *New*

York Times, at the time he was making *Marathon Man*. "You don't get rich if you're into that terribly noble, sacrificial kick."[4] Olivier, in fact, was happy to be working at all. At the time, in 1976, he was battling his third serious illness within an eight-year period. "I had to turn things down for more than a year because of my gorgeous, lovely, smashing illness, which is the worst I've ever had, just because it is so mysterious. I mean, cancer was one thing. I just treated it very rough and hardened my mind against it. Then, three years later, came the thrombosis. . . . They told me I couldn't act for twelve months, but I was on the stage again in four! I have a most extraordinary resilience; I always have had. . . . I got bored asking the eternal question, 'When will I feel well enough to work?,' so I decided to take a big risk and do it, knowing I'd have to pass a medical and take the chance of failing and having it buzzed all over that I had failed and was finished. I just barely scraped past the test, but I think from that moment, I began to feel better."[2]

Delighted to be at work again, Olivier accepted big roles in glossy Hollywood films. Not for the first time, he was accused of slumming; but surely, after such a distinguished record, after having established his dedication to the classics over popular culture, Olivier has earned the right, in this twilight of his career, to "go Hollywood"? His roles in both *Marathon Man* and *The Betsy*, moreover, do not depend on conventional star glamour, on "behaving" rather than "acting." Olivier was drawn to the two parts precisely for their acting opportunities: the chance they offered to work again on accents, to experiment with makeup, to create startling masks that his audience has never seen him wear in quite the same way before. The two roles, in short, are showcases for Olivier's continuing and undiminished relish to prove, even to flaunt, his versatility.

In the enormously popular *Marathon Man*, Olivier plays a former Nazi doctor lured to New York from his South American exile in order to claim jewels. The film's ethics are questionable, since the story uses the horrors of Nazi Germany as a background for standard thriller material about a series of complicated deceptions and double dealings. Though, under the circumstances, he can hardly create a deep characterization, his shallowness is artful: his doctor is a cold-eyed Nazi sadist, his face frozen in a perpetual sneer, his voice, with its strange slurring rhythms, its deliberate insinuating lowness, its edge of breathiness, capable of instilling instant terror. Working against the Grand Guignol conception of the role as written, Olivier plays the fiend with calm and restraint, with a kind of deadpan subtlety. In its absolute chilliness, the characterization recalls his work as the demotic Crassus in *Spartacus*. The role is no more than a stereotypical portrait of a Nazi, and unlike a Method actor, Olivier does not probe for psychological truth, for shading and nuance: he acts in a deliberately restricted, almost monochromatic range, playing it all for surface values.

He plays another hateful, power-mad character in *The Betsy*, a film version of Harold Robbins's idiotic saga of an automobile family. Perhaps because Olivier was his star, the director (Daniel Petrie) does not meet the tawdry potboiler material on its own level; mistakenly, the film aspires to class, with the result that this fantasy, written in the popular Robbins mold of letting the masses in on what the rich and famous are really like, lacks the good-natured vulgarity and flamboyance of the best of the overblown Hollywood melodramas like *The Other Side of Midnight* and *The Oscar*. *The Betsy* takes itself too seriously to become the transcendent kitsch that these other two films are.

Olivier himself, however, far from behaving like a great actor trapped in distasteful surroundings, gives a raunchy, low-down performance, meeting the trashy material head on. He isn't too proud to appear in a film that almost any other performer of his legendary stature would consider degrading. As Vincent Canby wrote in the *New York Times*, Olivier gives "one of the wittiest . . . comic performances of his long career, a demonstration that recalls bits and pieces of some of his greatest accomplishments, including *Richard III* and George Hurstwood in *Carrie*. . . . He doesn't pretend to be discovering the interior life of the character, which would certainly be the last thing Harold Robbins wanted or that Robbins could have brought off. Olivier's performance is all show, all surface mannerisms that are the cinematic equivalent to the kind of prose that Robbins writes. . . ."[3]

As the patriarch of an auto dynasty, Olivier has one of those roles of a dominant, larger-than-life character that have been the backbone of his career. The tycoon, who nurses a comeback hope in the form of a new kind of car (named "The Betsy," after his favorite great grand-daughter), is a feisty, cantankerous robber baron, a rule-breaker who flaunted decorum by having an affair with his daughter-in-law because his effeminate son proved an unworthy scion. He is a macho magnate, bewitched by his own sexual and personal magnetism. The absurd part is conceived in the same cliché-ridden fashion as the Nazi in *Marathon Man*, and again, Olivier shrewdly plays for superficial effects.

Told in a splintered *Godfather* fashion, the story moves back and forth between the present and the past, and requires Olivier to age from forty to ninety. Physically, he is convincing as both a vigorous nonagenarian, decked out in a white summer suit, his hair a shock of white, and as a handsome man of ripe middle age, a romantic figure capable of attracting a beautiful young woman by his energy and aura of power. In moving from middle to old age, Olivier changes the way he uses his body without resorting to caricature. He is not as successful vocally, however. He has made a characteristically conscientious attempt at a foreign accent—here, it's a Midwestern drawl. Typically, he hasn't cultivated beautiful tones; his voice is often harsh and grating, with a gravelly quality that he did not intend to be pleasing. Part of Olivier's daring has always included the freedom *not* to sound like a distinguished classical actor. Yet here the accent, studiously worked at, grates on American ears as an unconvincing hybrid. In the course of the film, Olivier has to say the word "car" many times, and so uncertain is his "r" sound that the word is given many different and contradictory pronunciations. Olivier's accents have always tended to be fanciful, even when he may have been trying for scrupulous imitation. The bizarre accent he adopts for *Marathon Man* is appropriate, though surely not, in any strict sense, "accurate." To American audiences, there is something lopsided in the way Olivier sounds in trying to talk like an American tycoon.

Though his performance is not entirely successful, it certainly has bravado and is evidence of exceedingly good sportmanship. Under the circumstances, this is a heroically straight-faced performance, with only a twinkle or an inflection now and again, and echoes of the wonderfully dry humor that is an Olivier trademark, to note the actor's true opinion of the material.

As of this writing, Olivier is starring in yet another pop thriller, Ira Levin's *The Boys from Brazil*, and has been signed to costar as the doctor in *Dracula*. He now seems, then, to be interested in the big, popular movies that he consistently refused ever since he left Hollywood to return to England during the war, and his late-in-the-day appearance in these blockbusters provides further evidence of his delight in variety and in confounding audience expectations. As a performer, Olivier has always avoided the predictable, and these starring parts in Hollywood trash provide a sly counterpoint to his august reputation as a classical actor.

Olivier play-acting with Michael Caine in *Sleuth* (1972).

9

Olivier's Achievement

WHEN PRESENTED AT THE NATIONAL THEATRE IN 1964, Olivier's monumental performance as Othello evoked comparisons with the nineteenth-century tradition of the egocentric tragic actor. Olivier's name was linked with Henry Irving and Edmund Kean, and his controversial, virtuoso Othello sealed his connection to the great romantic tradition in British acting. From his hot-blooded, unconventional Romeo in 1935 to his severe and unsentimental Shylock in 1970, Olivier's record in classical theater is unparalleled in the twentieth century. His interpretations of many of Shakespeare's heroes and villains, kings and clowns, have been consistently adventurous. He has offered novel and complex readings of, among others, Macbeth, Malvolio, Titus Andronicus, Hamlet, Lear, Coriolanus, Hotspur, and Richard III. In non-Shakespearean roles, his Oedipus, Astrov (in *Uncle Vanya*), Edgar (in *The Dance of Death*), Tyrone (in *Long Day's Journey into Night*), Mr. Puff (in *The Critic*), Sir Peter Teazle (in *The School for Scandal*), and Archie Rice (in *The Entertainer*) have been outstanding. For originality, daring, presence, and mastery of technique, he is clearly the foremost actor of his generation.

Among his roster of now-legendary performances, his Richard III and his Othello are the most spectacular. These two powerful characters inspired Olivier to his greatest technical accomplishments. These two parts are his most complete disguises and represent, therefore, the epitome of the kind of self-transformation that Olivier has always maintained as one of his chief aims as an actor. For his satanic Richard and coal-black, swaggering Othello, he radically altered his voice, his use of his body, and the contours of his face. But these spectacularly crafted performances, in which he buried himself beneath the masks he created for his characters, are

163

Olivier as Hamlet (1948), after the play scene (with Norman Wooland as Horatio).

not simply displays of technical ingenuity; they are incisive character portraits, probing examinations of characters whose extraordinary pride, ambition, fears, and jealousies have universal significance and application. Olivier's Richard and his Othello contain aspects of Everyman, and it is exactly to the degree that he reveals the characters' scarred and battered humanity that his work achieves profound levels.

At his most magnificent—as Richard, Othello, Oedipus, Archie Rice—Olivier is not simply a brilliant technician who can change his appearance and his voice to suit the character, he is an inspired student of human psychology whose strongest work, like that of all great creative and imaginative artists, reveals universal truths about the nature of man and his world.

The Olivier style is filled with tantalizing contradictions. Beginning with an almost childlike interest in disguise and artifice, the actor probes deeply into his characters; putting on a mask himself, he unmasks the people he plays. Olivier distrusts the Method actor's improvisations and his egocentric self-analysis, his use of acting as a kind of neurotic transference; yet Olivier's impersonal, objective technique, which begins with external details, produces characterizations that are as gnarled, as intimate and densely psychological, as the best of those that result from the Method.

For all his mastery of disguise, however, his fascination with illusion and appearance, Olivier is not infinitely malleable. He is better at playing leaders than followers; he is more adept at comedy than tragedy; and there are mannerisms of voice and movement and gesture that are visible from performance to performance. Though he always tries to hide himself, there are yet-lingering signs of the man beneath the performer's masquerades.

Films have the added advantage over theater of preserving a record of the actor's performance, and Olivier's film work, from his novice period in the early 1930s to his latest starring roles in garish Hollywood melodramas, provides a rich demonstration of his development. Contrary to popular belief, Olivier did not start out with genius, or even with unusual gifts. He had imagination and energy, but little depth and a light voice that needed much work. But he accepted the challenge, and he trained like an athlete, building his voice, deepening its range and color and expressiveness, just as he developed his originally scrawny physique.

In film, as on stage, his acting has been both bombastic and understated, both theatrical and naturalistic. Sometimes he has paraded his technique, and his evident joy in acting is a kind of exuberant showing-off; sometimes he conceals his method, erasing entirely the hamminess that has often been a basic part of his persona as eminent classical actor. The films that were made simply to preserve some of his most acclaimed stage performances—*Uncle Vanya, The Dance of Death, Othello,* even to some extent *The Entertainer*—cannot contain the full passion of the original interpretations; Olivier's theatrical fire is apparent, though necessarily somewhat muffled. As Kenneth Tynan, the most astute critic of his work, has written, Olivier needs the kind of absolute control over his performance and his audience that is available only to a stage actor. While the full force of his energy, his startling *presence*, as a performer can be savored completely only in the theater, Olivier developed into a skillful film actor, and the roles he created *for* film (as opposed to the transcriptions of stage work) constitute a substantial achievement.

In its versatility, its risks, its display of bravura technique, in fact, Olivier's film record almost matches his accomplishment in theater. In film, as in the theater, he has moved from classics to popular material, from period pieces to contemporary dramas, from romantic matinee idol to character actor in heavy disguise, from larger-than-life hero to down-and-out victim.

His main contribution to films, though, is not as an actor but as a director. His three Shakespearean adaptations—his *Henry V, Hamlet,* and *Richard III*—introduced Shakespeare to millions of moviegoers and proved that theatrical convention and cinematic realism can be mutually reinforcing. His three films are among the most intelligent and fluent of all film adaptations from other sources. Though *Henry V* was the real landmark, being the first time that Shakespeare comfortably inhabited the film frame, all three productions are major achievements that belong in the select company of the world's great films.

"Of all the things I've done in my life," Olivier said in an interview for the BBC in 1971, "directing a motion picture is the most beautiful. It's the most exciting and the nearest that an interpretive craftsman, such as an actor . . . can possibly get to being a creator." Perhaps for him as well as for us, the major disappointment of Olivier's career has been that, apart from his direction of the minor *Prince and the Showgirl* in 1957 and the theaterbound *Three Sisters* in 1970, his directorial canon is limited to the three Shakespearean films. As a director working in what was for him a new medium, Olivier indicated extraordinary sensitivity to the texture and rhythm of films. In addition to his skillful handling of actors, he proved highly sophisticated in his composition of images, his use of camera movement and camera placement, his transitions in time and place, his pacing, and his creation of mood and atmosphere. We certainly had the right to expect more from Olivier as a director of films, and yet, because of his bitter disappointment in being unable to finance a long-planned film of *Macbeth*, because realist trends in British films made Shakespearean adaptations seem old-fashioned and uncommercial, because no producer like Fillipo del Guidice or Alexander Korda came forward to prod Olivier to attempt further projects, he abandoned film directing in order to devote his primary energies to superintending the fortunes of the National Theatre. His inability to become a major and continuing directorial force in the British and international film industry must count as a major lapse in a career of exceptional fullness.

Because of age and health, it is unlikely that Olivier will be able to sustain the rigors of directing another film, and it is equally unlikely that he will be able to give us a true theatrical swan song—an awesome Lear, for instance, or a majestic Prospero (one of the few major Shakespearean roles he has never attempted, and one that is, of course, a perfect vehicle for a gala farewell). Because it is in his blood, he will, however, continue to act whenever and wherever he can—on film and television, on recordings and radio. He is always capable of surprising us, but it is likely that his major achievements are behind him; it is improbable that there will be another performance of the magnitude of his Richard or Othello. Olivier's contribution to theater and films is an achievement of permanent value, and whatever he is willing or able to offer us now ought to be taken, gratefully, as adornments to the official record.

"If I wasn't an actor, I think I'd have gone mad," Olivier said in a BBC interview in 1975. "You have to have some extra voltage, some extra temperament to reach certain heights. Art is a little bit larger than life—it's an exaltation of life—and I think you probably need a little touch of madness." For more than fifty years, throughout a truly distinguished "life in the theater," he has generously shared with us that "voltage," that "exaltation," that "touch of madness."

Notes and References

Preface

1. Olivier talking to Kenneth Tynan, BBC television interview, June 23, 1967.
2. *Ibid.*
3. Quoted in *Logan Gourlay,* ed., *Olivier* (New York, 1974), p. 45.
4. Olivier talking to Kenneth Tynan, in *Great Acting,* ed. by Hal Burton (New York, 1967), p. 114.
5. Introduction to *Othello. The National Theatre Production* (New York, 1967), p. 4.

Chapter One

1. Felix Barker, *The Oliviers* (Philadelphia, 1953), p. 26.
2. John Cottrell, *Laurence Olivier* (Englewood Cliffs, New Jersey, 1975), p. 151.
3. Olivier talking to Kenneth Tynan, BBC interview, 1967, quoted in Cottrell, p. 20.
4. Cottrell, p. 44.
5. Barker, p. 85.
6. *Saturday Review of Literature,* May 25, 1946, pp. 27–28.
7. Cottrell, p. 2.
8. Gourlay, p. 186.
9. Tyrone Guthrie, *A Life in the Theatre* (New York, 1959), p. 186.
10. *Ibid.,* p. 187.
11. *Ibid.*
12. *Dramatis Personae* (New York, 1963). pp. 206–208.
13. Olivier talking to Harold Hobson, *Sunday Times Weekly Review,* London, November 3, 1963.
14. Cottrell, p. 140.
15. *Ibid.*

16. *Othello. The National Theatre Production,* p. 2.

17. Quoted in *Great Acting,* p. 7.

Chapter Two

1. Olivier, quoted in *The New York Times,* January 4, 1940.

2. *Graham Greene on Film* (New York, 1972), p. 100.

3. Tynan, *Curtains* (New York, 1961), p. 10.

4. Information about Vivien Leigh's emotional problems derived from Anne Edwards, *Vivien Leigh* (New York, 1977).

Chapter Three

1. All quoted in Harry Geduld, *Filmguide to Henry V* (Bloomington, Indiana, 1973), pp. 67–68.

2. *Agee on Film* (Boston, 1964), pp. 211–12.

Chapter Four

1. Roger Furse, "Designing the Film *Hamlet,*" in *Hamlet. The Film and the Play,* ed. by Alan Dent (London, 1948), n.p.

2. Sir Laurence Olivier, "Foreword," *Ibid.,* n.p.

3. Jack J. Jorgens, *Shakespeare on Film* (Bloomington, 1977), p. 213.

4. Furse, "Designing the Film *Hamlet.*"

5. Jorgens, p. 215

6. BBC Interview, June 23, 1967.

7. Olivier, "Foreword" to *Hamlet. The Film and the Play.*

8. "Text-editing Shakespeare, with Particular Reference to *Hamlet,*" in *Hamlet. The Film and the Play,* n.p.

9. "A Prince of Shreds and Patches," *Mary McCarthy's Theatre Chronicles 1937–1962* (New York, 1963), p. 144.

10. *Ibid.,* p. 141.

11. Bernard Grebanier, *Then Came Each Actor* (New York, 1975, p. 331.

12. *Agee on Film,* pp. 388–89.

Chapter Five

1. Jorgens, p. 146.

2. Roger Manvell, *Shakespeare and the Film* (New York, 1971), p. 48.

3. Olivier talking to Kenneth Tynan, quoted in *Great Acting,* p. 25.

4. Tynan, Introduction to Othello. The National Theatre Production, p. 2.

5. *New York Times,* March 12, 1956, p. 1.

Chapter Six

1. André Bazin, "Theatre and Cinema," *What Is Cinema?,* I:105, 107.

2. Terence Rattigan in *Olivier,* ed. Logan Gourlay, pp. 130–31.

3. Gourlay, p. 194.
4. Gourlay, pp. 192, 193.

Chapter Seven

1. Introduction to *Othello*, pp. 1–2.
2. Tynan talking to Olivier, quoted in *Great Acting*, p. 28.
3. *The Player Kings* (New York, 1971), p. 229.

Chapter Eight

1. Olivier talking to Jim Watters, *New York Times* (October 16, 1976).
2. *Ibid.*
3. *New York Times*, February 26, 1978.

Selected Bibliography

Books

BALL, ROBERT HAMILTON. *Shakespeare on Silent Film*. New York: Theatre Arts Books. Exhaustive, humorless study of an impossible subject—Shakespeare without words.

BARKER, FELIX. *The Oliviers*. Philadelphia: J. B. Lippincott, 1953. Adulatory early biography, with much solid information.

BETTS, ERNEST. *The Film Business. A History of British Cinema 1896–1972*. New York: Pitman, 1973. Superficial, chatty history, with useful factual information along the way.

BILLINGTON, MICHAEL. *The Modern Actor*. London: Hamish Hamilton, 1973. Intelligent analysis of Olivier's heroic style.

COTTRELL, JOHN. *Laurence Olivier*. New Jersey: Prentice-Hall, 1975. Definitive biography. A sensible, balanced assessment of both the private man and his public career.

DARLINGTON, W. A. *Laurence Olivier*. London: Morgan Grampian, 1968. Glowing appreciation of Olivier on stage.

DENT, ALAN, ed. *Hamlet. The Film and the Play*. London: World Film Publications, Ltd., 1948. Useful comparisons, good introductory essays.

————. *Vivien Leigh: A Bouquet*. London: Hamish Hamilton, 1969. Glamorized and polite. Entirely superseded by Anne Edwards's hard-hitting biography.

DONALDSON, FRANCES. *The Actor-Managers*. Chicago: Henry Regnery, 1970. Pleasantly written history of the great actor-manager tradition of the nineteenth century, a tradition to which Olivier aspired without conspicuous success.

DURGNAT, RAYMOND. *A Mirror for England. British Movies from Austerity to Affluence*. New York: Praeger, 1971. Lively, idiosyncratic discussion of British films covering the period of Olivier's film activity.

ECKERT, CHARLES W. *Focus on Shakespearean Films*. Englewood Cliffs, New Jersey: Prentice-Hall, 1972. Fine collection of essays and reviews;

Mary McCarthy's characteristically incisive review of Olivier's *Hamlet* and Constance Brown's essay on visual imagery in Olivier's *Richard III* are of particular interest, though the entire collection is useful.

EDWARDS, ANNE. *Vivien Leigh*. New York: Simon and Schuster, 1977. Harrowing biography of the actress. Olivier is presented as patient husband of a psychotic.

FAIRWEATHER, VIRGINIA. *Cry God for Larry*. London: Calder & Boyars, 1969. Chatty, superficial account (by Olivier's secretary) of backstage problems during Olivier's period as director of the National Theatre.

FINDLATER, RICHARD. *The Player Kings*. New York: Stein and Day, 1971. Intelligent discussions of England's great actors, from Garrick to Olivier and Gielgud. Presents Olivier's career in the context of the great tradition in British acting and draws telling comparisons between Olivier's romanticism and Gielgud's classicism.

GEDULD, HARRY M. *Filmguide to Henry V*. Bloomington, Indiana: Indiana University Press, 1973. The most complete discussion in print on the landmark film. Useful production details, and thorough structural analysis.

GIELGUD, JOHN. *Early Stages*. New York: Macmillan, 1939. Good discussion of the author's 1935 *Romeo and Juliet*, and astute comparisons between the author's technique and Olivier's.

GREBANIER, BERNARD. *Then Came Each Actor*. New York: McKay, 1975. Opinionated, breezily written history of Shakespearean acting. Unfriendly to Olivier, who is criticized for indulgence and mannerism.

GOURLAY, LOGAN, ed. *Olivier*. New York: Stein and Day, 1974. Excellent collection of interviews in which actors, directors, and playwrights discuss and summarize Olivier's accomplishments, his strengths and weaknesses, his temperament off stage and on, his technical resources. Provides a series of rich close-ups of the actor's entire career.

GUTHRIE, TYRONE. *A Life in the Theatre*. New York: McGraw-Hill, 1959. Good, if casual, observations of Olivier's early Shakespearean performances.

JORGENS, JACK J. *Shakespeare on Film*. Bloomington, Indiana: Indiana Press, 1977. The finest discussion of the subject. Beautifully written, and sustained by the author's cheering belief that films and Shakespeare are a good and potentially enriching combination.

KULIK, KAROL. *Alexander Korda. The Man Who Could Work Miracles*. New Rochelle, New York: Arlington House, 1975. Thorough account of the producer's career.

MANVELL, ROGER. *Shakespeare and the Film*. New York: Praeger, 1971. Some valuable interview material with Olivier, but superficial analysis of the films.

SPEAIGHT, ROBERT. *Shakespeare on the Stage*. Boston: Little, Brown, 1973. Beautifully illustrated, popular history of Shakespeare in performance. Olivier's innovative approach to Shakespeare given full value.

TABORI, PAUL. *Alexander Korda*. London: Oldbourne, 1959. Useful biography. The Oliviers have supporting roles.
TREWIN, J. C. *The Birmingham Repertory Theatre, 1913–1963*. London: Barrie and Rockliff, 1963. Basic history of the theater where Olivier's first Shakespearean performances were given.
TYNAN, KENNETH, ed. *Othello. The National Theatre Production*. New York: Stein and Day, 1967. Excellent short introduction, "Othello: The Actor and the Moor," by one of the actor's most stringent and most appreciative critics, describes Olivier's arduous preparation for the role.
WALKER, ALEXANDER. *Hollywood. UK. The British Film Industry in the Sixties*. New York: Stein and Day, 1974. Excellent discussions of the British Free Cinema and kitchen-sink realism.

2. Parts of Books

AGEE, JAMES. *Agee on Film*. Boston: Beacon Press, 1964, pp. 207–12, 361–66, 388–92. Definitive contemporary reviews of *Henry V* and *Hamlet*.
BAZIN, ANDRÉ. *What is Cinema? Volume I*. Berkeley: University of California Press, 1974. Bazin's brilliant essay, "Theatre and Cinema," pp. 76–124, includes many appreciative references to Olivier's adaptations.
BURTON, HAL, ed. *Great Acting*. New York: Hill and Wang, 1967. Olivier's interview with Kenneth Tynan, pp. 11–32, offers many perceptive and honest self-appraisals.

Filmography

1. Films Directed by Laurence Olivier

(Briefer accounts of other pictures in which Olivier played follow in Part 2)

HENRY V (Two Cities–United Artists, 1945)
Producer and Director: Laurence Olivier
Screenplay: Laurence Olivier, Alan Dent and Reginald Beck from the play
 by William Shakespeare
Cinematographer: Robert Krasker
Art Directors: Paul Sheriff, Roger Furse
Music: William Walton
Sound: John Dennis, Desmond Dew
Editors: Laurence Olivier and Reginald Beck
Cast: Laurence Olivier (King Henry V of England), Renee Asherson (Prin-
 cess Katherine), Robert Newton (Ancient Pistol), Leslie Banks
 (Chorus), Esmond Knight (Fluellen), Leo Genn (The Constable of
 France), Felix Aylmer (The Archbishop of Canterbury), Ralph Truman
 (Mountjoy), Harcourt Williams (King Charles VI of France)
Running Time: 127 minutes
New York Premiere: June 17, 1946, City Center
16mm. rental: Contemporary–McGraw-Hill and others

HAMLET (Two Cities–Universal, 1948)
Producer and Director: Laurence Olivier
Associate Producer: Reginald Beck
Assistant Producer: Anthony Bushnell
Assistant Director: Peter Bolton
Screenplay: Alan Dent from Shakespeare's tragedy
Cinematographer: Desmond Dickenson
Art Director: Carmen Dillon
Set Decoration: Roger Ramsdell
Costumes: Elizabeth Hennings

175

Sound: John W. Mitchell and Harry Miller
Special Effects: Paul Sheriff, Henry Harris, Jack Whitehead
Music: William Walton
Editor: Helga Cranston
Cast: Laurence Olivier (Hamlet), Eileen Herbie (Queen Gertrude), Basil
    Sydney (King Claudius), Jean Simmons (Ophelia), Felix Aylmer
    (Polonius) Norman Wooland (Horatio, Terence Morgan (Laertes),
    Stanley Holloway (Gravedigger)
Running Time: 160 minutes
New York Premiere: September 29, 1948, under the auspices of the Thea-
    ter Guild
16mm. rental: Contemporary–McGraw-Hill and others.

RICHARD III (Laurence Olivier Productions–London Films, 1955)
Producer and Director: Laurence Olivier
Associate Director: Anthony Bushnell
Screenplay: Adapted from the play by William Shakespeare
Cinematographer: Otto Heller
Art Director: Carmen Dillon
Costumes: L & H Mathan, Ltd.
Music: Sir William Walton
Special Effects: Wally Veevers
Editor: Helga Cranston
Cast: Laurence Olivier (King Richard III), John Gielgud (Duke of Clar-
    ence), Ralph Richardson (Duke of Buckingham), Alec Clunes (Duke of
    Hastings), Claire Bloom (Lady Anne), Sir Cedric Hardwicke (King
    Edward IV), Pamela Brown (Jane Shore), Mary Kennedy (Queen
    Elizabeth), Norman Wooland (Catesby)
Running Time: 158 minutes
New York Premiere: March 11, 1956, Bijou (the film was also shown on the
    same day in a special program on national NBC television from 2:30 to
    5:30 P.M.)
16mm. rental: Janus Films

THE PRINCE AND THE SHOWGIRL (Warner Brothers, 1957)
Producer and Director: Laurence Olivier
Executive Producer: Hugh Perceval
Associate Director: Anthony Bushnell
Assistant Director: David Ortor
Screenplay: Terence Rattigan, from his play *The Sleeping Prince*
Cinematographer: Jack Cardiff
Art Director: Carmen Dillon
Set Decorator: Davis Simoni
Costumes: Beatrice Dawson

Music: Richard Addinsell
Sound: John Mitchell and Gordon McCallum
Special Effects: Bill Warrington and Charles Staffel
Editor: Jack Harris
Cast: Laurence Olivier (Grand Duke Charles), Marilyn Monroe (Elsie), Sybil Thorndyke (The Queen Dowager), Richard Wattis (Northbrook), Jeremy Spenser (King Nicholas)
Running Time: 117 minutes
New York Premiere: May 10, 1957, Radio City Music Hall
16mm. rental: MacMillan/Audio Brandon and others

THREE SISTERS (American Film Theatre, 1970)
Producer: Alan Lore
Associate Producers: Timothy Burrill, James C. Katz
Co-director: John Sichel
Assistant Director: Simon Relph
Screenplay: Based on a production of the play of the same title by Anton Chekhov
Translation and special research: Moura Budberg
Cinematographer: Geoffrey Unsworth
Art Director: Bill Hutchinson
Production Designer: Josef Svoboda
Costumes: Beatrice Dawson
Music: Sir William Walton (additional music by Derek Hudson and Gary Hughes)
Editor: Jack Harris
Cast: Laurence Olivier (Dr. Chebutikin), Joan Plowright (Masha), Jeanne Watts (Olga), Louise Purnell (Irina), Derek Jacobi (Andrei), Alan Bates (Vershinin)
Running Time: 165 minutes
New York Premiere: See Note below
16mm. rental or lease: United Films, Tulsa, Oklahoma.
(Note: This was one of a series of films that were released simultaneously in 512 theaters throughout the United States and Canada for two-day-only subscription showings in 1973–74. This experiment ended with its second season.)

2. Other Films in Which Sir Laurence Olivier Appeared

TOO MANY CROOKS (Fox, 1930)
Produced and directed by George King: screenplay by Billie Bristow from a story by Basil Roscoe (38 minutes)
Cast: Laurence Olivier (The Man), Dorothy Boyd (The Girl), A. Bromley Davenport (The Man Upstairs), Arthur Stratton (The Burglar), Ellen Pollack (Rose), Mina Burnett (The Maid)

THE TEMPORARY WIDOW (UFA, 1930—Made in Germany, released in the United States under the title *Murder for Sale*)
Producer: Erich Pommer; Director, Gustav Ucicky; Screenplay, Karl Hartl, Walter Reisch, and Benn W. Levy from Curt Goetz's play *Hokuspokus* (84 minutes)
Cast: Lillian Harvey (Kitty Keller), Laurence Olivier (Peter Billie), Athole Stewart (President Grant)

FRIENDS AND LOVERS (RKO-Radio, 1931)
Directed by Victor Schertzinger, adapted from a novel by Maurice de Kobra (68 minutes)
Cast: Adolphe Menjou (Captain Roberts), Lili Damita (Alva Sangrito), Laurence Olivier (Lt. Nichols), Erich von Stroheim (Victor Sangrito), Hugh Herbert (McNellis)
16mm. rental: Films, Inc.

POTIPHAR'S WIFE (British International Pictures—First National–Pathé, 1931; American title: *Her Strange Desire*)
Directed by Maurice Elvey from a screenplay by Edgar C. Middleton (78 minutes)
Cast: Nora Swinburne (Lady Diana Bromford), Laurence Olivier (Straker)

THE YELLOW PASSPORT (Fox, 1931; American title: *The Yellow Ticket*)
Directed by Raoul Walsh, from the play by Michael Borton
Cast: Elissa Landi, Lionel Barrymore, Laurence Olivier, Boris Karloff, Walter Byron

WESTWARD PASSAGE (RKO-Radio, 1932)
Directed by Robert Milton, from a novel by Margaret Ayer Barnes
Cast: Ann Harding (Olivia Van Tyre), Laurence Olivier (Nick Allen), Juliette Compton (Henriette), Zasu Pitts (Mrs. Turesdale)

NO FUNNY BUSINESS (F.P.I., 1933)
Produced by Jim Stafford and directed by Stafford and Victor Hanbury, from a story by Dorall Hope
Cast: Gertrude Lawrence, Laurence Olivier, Jill Esmond

PERFECT UNDERSTANDING (United Artists, 1933)
Produced by Gloria Swanson Pictures Corporation; directed by Cyril Gardner, from a screenplay by Miles Malleson
Cast: Gloria Swanson (Judy), Laurence Olivier (Nicholas Randall), John Halliday (Ronnson), Sir Nigel Playfair (Lord Portleigh), Michael Farmer (George)

MOSCOW NIGHTS (London Films—Capital, 1935; American title: *I Stand Condemned*)
Produced by Alexander Korda, Alexis Granowski, and Max Schach; directed by Anthony Asquith, from a screenplay by Erich Seipman, based on Pierre Benoit's novel *Les Nuits de Moscow* (75 minutes)
Cast: Harry Baur (Brioukow), Laurence Olivier (Capt. Ignatoff), Penelope Dudley Ward (Natasha)
16mm. rental: Kit Parker Films, Carmel Valley, CA 93924; 16mm. sales, Cinema 8, Chester, CT 06412

AS YOU LIKE IT (Twentieth Century–Fox, 1936)
Produced and Directed by Paul Czinner: screenplay by Robert J. Cullen from the play by William Shakespeare: music by William Walton (96 minutes)
Cast: Elisabeth Bergner (Rosalind), Laurence Olivier (Orlando), Henry Ainley (the banished Duke), Sophie Stewart (Celia), Mackenzie Ward (Touchstone)
16mm. rental: Twyman Films, Dayton, Ohio, and others; 16mm. sales, Blackhawk Films, Davenport, Iowa 52808

CONQUEST OF THE AIR (United Artists, 1936)
Produced by Alexander Korda; directed by Zoltan Korda and others; screenplay by Hugh Gray and Peter Bezencenet, based on a story by John Monk Saunders (71 minutes)
Cast: Laurence Olivier (Vincent Lunardi), Henry Victor (Otto Lilienthal), John Turnball (von Zeppelin)

TWENTY-ONE DAYS (Columbia, 1937, released in the United States in 1940 with the title *Twenty-One Days Together*).
Produced by Alexander Korda; directed by Basil Dean, from a screenplay by Graham Greene based on a play by John Galsworthy (75 minutes).
Cast: Vivien Leigh (Wanda), Laurence Olivier (Larry Durant), Leslie Banks (Keith Durrant), Francis L. Sullivan (Mander)

FIRE OVER ENGLAND (United Artists, 1936)
Produced by Erich Pommer; directed by William K. Howard, from a screenplay by Clemence Dane and Sergei Nolbandov, based on the novel of the same title by A. E. W. Mason; cinematography by James Wong Howe (88 minutes)
16mm. rental: Janus Films, Budget Films; 8mm. sales: Milestone Movies, Monroe, Conn.

THE DIVORCE OF LADY X (United Artists, 1938)
Produced by Alexander Korda; directed by Tim Wheelan; screenplay by

Lajor Biro and Robert Sherwood from Biro's play *Counsel's Opinion;*
music by Miklos Rosza (90 minutes).
Cast: Laurence Olivier (Logan), Merle Oberon (Leslie), Binnie Barnes
(Lady Mere), Ralph Richardson (Lord Mere)
16mm. rental: Mogull's, New York, NY.

WUTHERING HEIGHTS (Samuel Goldwyn–United Artists, 1939)
Produced by Samuel Goldwyn; directed by William Wyler; screenplay by
Ben Hecht and Charles MacArthur from the novel by Emily Bronte;
cinematography by Gregg Toland (103 minutes)
Cast: Merle Oberon (Cathy Earnshaw), Laurence Olivier (Heathcliff),
David Niven (Edgar Linton), Flora Robson (Ellen Dean), Donald
Crisp (Dr. Kenneth), Hugh Williams (Hudley), Geraldine Fitzgerald
(Isabella Linton), Leo G. Carroll (Joseph)
16mm. rental: MacMillan/Audio Brandon

Q PLANES (Columbia, 1939; American release title: *Clouds Over Europe*)
Produced by Alexander Korda and Irving Asher; directed by Tim
Wheelan, from a screenplay by Ian Dalrymple (82 minutes)
Cast: Laurence Olivier (Tony McVane), Valerie Hobson (Kay Hammond),
Ralph Richardson (Charles Hammond), George Curzon (Jenkins)
16mm. rental: United Productions of America, 145 East 49th St., New
York, NY 10017

PRIDE AND PREJUDICE (Metro-Goldwyn-Mayer, 1940)
Produced by Hunt Stromberg; directed by Robert Z. Leonard; screenplay
by Aldous Huxley and Jane Murfin from Helen Jerome's dramatization
of Jane Austen's novel (117 minutes)
Cast: Greer Garson (Elizabeth Bennet), Laurence Olivier (Mr. Darcy),
Mary Boland (Mrs. Bennet), Edna Mae Oliver (Lady Catherine),
Maurine O'Sullivan (Jane Bennet), Ann Rutherford (Lydia Bennet),
Heather Angel (Kitty Bennet), Marsha Hunt (Mary Bennet), Edmund
Gwenn (Mr. Bennet)
16mm. rental: Films, Inc.

REBECCA (Selznick International–United Artists, 1940)
Produced by David O. Selznick; directed by Alfred Hitchcock; screenplay
by Robert E. Sherwood and Joan Harrison from Dauphne du Maurier's
novel of the same title (130 minutes)
Cast: Laurence Olivier (Maxim de Winter), Joan Fontaine (Mrs. de
Winter), George Sanders (Jack Favell), Judith Anderson (Mrs. Danvers), Nigel Bruce (Major Giles Lucy), Gladys Cooper (Beatrice), Flor-

ence Bates (Mrs. Van Hopper), Reginald Denny (Crawley), C. Aubrey
Smith (Major Julyan)
16mm. rental: MacMillan/Audio Brandon and others

LADY HAMILTON (United Artists, 1941; American release title: *That
Hamilton Woman*)
Produced and Directed by Alexander Korda, from a screenplay by R. C.
Sheriff and Walter Reisch (124 minutes)
Cast: Laurence Olivier (Admiral Lord Nelson), Vivien Leigh (Lady Emma
Hamilton), Gladys Cooper (Lady Nelson), Sara Allgood (Mrs. Cada-
gon-Lyon), Henry Wilcox (Captain Hardy), Heather Angel (Street
Girl)
16mm. rental: Ivy Films

49TH. PARALLEL (Columbia, 1941; American release title, *The Invaders*)
Produced and directed by Michael Powell, from a screenplay by Rod-
ney Ackland and Emeric Pressburger (105 minutes)
Cast: Laurence Olivier (Johnnie, the Trapper), Finlay Currie (The Factor),
Glynis Johns (Anna), Leslie Howard (Philip Armstrong Scott),
Raymond Massey (Andy Brock), Eric Portman (Lt. Hirth)

THE DEMI-PARADISE (General Film Distributors, 1943; American re-
lease title: *Adventure for Two*).
Produced by Anatole de Grunwald and directed by Anthony Asquith from a
screenplay by de Grunwald (115 minutes)
Cast: Laurence Olivier (Ivan Dimitrievitch Kouznetsoff), Penelope Ward
(Ann Tidall), Margaret Rutherford (Rowena Ventnor)

CARRIE (Paramount, 1951)
Produced and directed by William Wyler, from a screenplay by Ruth and
Augustus Goetz, based on Theodore Dreiser's novel *Sister Carrie* (118
minutes)
Cast: Laurence Olivier (George Hurstwood), Jennifer Jones (Carrie
Meeber), Miriam Hopkins (Julie Hurstwood), Eddie Albert (Charles
Drouet), Basil Ruysdael (Mr. Fitzgerald)
16mm. rental: Janus Films

THE MAGIC BOX (Festival Film Productions, 1951)
Produced by Ronald Neame; directed by John Boulting; screenplay by Eric
Ambler from Ray Allister's novel *Friese-Greene* (118 minutes)
Cast: Robert Donat (William Friese-Greene), Margaret Johnston (Edith
Friese-Greene), Maria Schell (Helene Friese-Greene), Laurence
Olivier (PC 94 B)
16mm. rental and lease: United Films, Tulsa, Oklahoma

THE BEGGAR'S OPERA (Warner Brothers, 1953)
Produced by Laurence Olivier and Herbert Wilcox; directed by Peter
   Brook; screenplay by Dennis Canman, from an adaptation of John
   Gay's musical play *The Beggar's Opera* (1728) by Christopher Fry;
   music by Sir Arthur Bliss; opera sets and costumes by George
   Wakhevitch (94 minutes)
Cast: Laurence Olivier (MacHeath), Hugh Griffith (The Beggar), Dorothy
   Tutin (Polly Peachum), George Devine (Peachum), Mary Clare (Mrs.
   Peachum), Stanley Holloway (Lockit), Daphne Anderson (Lucy)
16mm. rental: MacMillan/Audio Brandon and others

THE DEVIL'S DISCIPLE (United Artists, 1959)
Produced by Ben Hecht; directed by Guy Hamilton; screenplay by John
   Dishton and Roland Kibbee, from George Bernard Shaw's play of the
   same title (82 minutes)
Cast: Laurence Olivier (General "Gentleman Johnnie" Burgoyne), Burt
   Lancaster (Rev. Anthony Anderson), Kirk Douglas (Richard Dudgeon),
   Eva LeGalliene (Mrs. Dudgeon), Judith Anderson (Janet Scott)
16mm. rental: United Artists 16

SPARTACUS (Universal-International, 1960)
Executive Producer, Kirk Douglas; produced by Edward Lewis; directed
   by Stanley Kubrick; screenplay by Dalton Trumbo, from a novel of the
   same title by Howard Fast (190 minutes)
Cast: Kirk Douglas (Spartacus), Laurence Olivier (Crassus), Jean Simmons
   (Varinia), Charles Laughton (Gracchus), Peter Ustinov (Batiatus), John
   Gavin (Julius Caesar), Nina Foch (Helena Glabrus), Tony Curtis (An-
   toninus)
16mm. rental: Universal 16, Twyman Films

THE ENTERTAINER (Bryanston-Continental, 1960)
Produced by Harry Saltzman; directed by Tony Richardson; screenplay by
   John Osborne and Nigel Kneale, based on Osborne's play of the same
   title (97 minutes)
Cast: Laurence Olivier (Archie Rice), Brenda DeBanzie (Phoebe Rice), Joan
   Plowright (Jean Rice), Roger Livesay (Billy Rice), Alan Bates (Frank
   Rice), Albert Finney (Mick Rice); McDonal Hobley (Himself)
16mm. rental: Walter Reade 16.

TERM OF TRIAL (Warner Brothers–Pathé–Romulus, 1962)
Produced by James Woolf; directed by Peter Glenville, from his own
   screenplay, based on a novel by James Barlow (130 minutes)
Cast: Laurence Olivier (Graham Weir), Simone Signoret (Anna), Roland

Culver (Trowman), Frank Pettingell (Ferguson), Sarah Miles (Shirley Taylor)

16mm. rental: Warner Brothers, Non-Theatrical Division

BUNNY LAKE IS MISSING (Columbia, 1965)

Produced and directed by Otto Preminger, from a screenplay by John and Penelope Mortimer, based on a novel by Evelyn Piper (107 minutes)

Cast: Sir Laurence Olivier (Newhouse), Carol Lynley (Ann), Keir Dullea (Steven), Noel Coward (Wilson)

16mm. rental: MacMillan/Audio Brandon

OTHELLO (B.H.E. Productions, 1966)

Produced by Anthony Havelock-Allan and John Bradbourne; directed by Stuart Burge, from the British National Theater production of William Shakespeare's play (170 minutes)

Cast: Laurence Olivier (Othello), Maggie Smith (Desdemona), Frank Finlay (Iago), Robert Lang (Roderigo), Joyce Redman (Emilia)

16mm. rental: Warner Brothers, Non-Theatrical Division

KHARTOUM (United Artists, 1966)

Produced by Julian Blaustein; directed by Basil Drearden and Yakim Canutt, from a screenplay by Robert Ardrey

Cast: Charlton Heston (Gordon), Laurence Olivier (The Mahdi), Richard Johnson (Col. Stewart), Ralph Richardson (Mr. Gladstone).

16mm. rental: United Artists 16; MacMillan/Audio/Brandon

THE DANCE OF DEATH (B.H.E.-Paramount, 1969)

Produced by Lord Brabourne and Anthony Havelocak-Allan; directed by David Giles; screenplay by C.D. Locock from August Strindberg's play of the same title (149 minutes)

Cast: Laurence Olivier (Army Captain), Geraldine McEwan (Wife), Robert Lang (Visitor)

THE SHOES OF THE FISHERMAN (Metro-Goldwyn-Mayer, 1968)

Produced by George Englund; directed by Michael Anderson; screenplay John Patrick and James Kennaway, based on a best-selling novel of the same title by Morris L. West; Music by Alex North (162 minutes)

Cast: Anthony Quinn (Pope Kiril), Laurence Olivier (Premier Kamenev), Oskar Werner (Father Telemond), David Janssen (George Faber), Vittorio DeSica (Cardinal Rinaldi)

16mm. rental: Films, Inc.

184   LAURENCE OLIVIER

BATTLE OF BRITAIN (United Artists, 1969)
Produced by Harry Saltzman and Benjamin Fisz; directed by Guy Hamilton, from a screenplay by James Kennaway and Wilfred Greatorey (130 minutes)
Cast: Laurence Olivier (Sir Hugh Dowding), Michael Caine (Squadron Leader Canfield), Trevor Howard (Air Officer Commanding No. 11 Group), Keith Park (Air Vice Marshall), Harry Andrews (Senior Civil Servant), Susannah York (Maggie Harvey)
16mm. rental: United Artists 16

OH! WHAT A LOVELY WAR (Paramount, 1969)
Produced by Brian Duffy and Richard Attenborough and directed by Attenborough; based on Joan Littlewood's revue of the same title
Cast: Laurence Olivier (Sir John French), Maggie Smith (Dance-Hall Hostess), John Gielgud (Count Von Berchtold), Ralph Richardson (Sir Edward Grey), John Rae (Grandpa Smith), Mary Wimbush (Mother Smith), Corin Redgrave (Bertie Smith)
16mm. rental: Films, Inc.

DAVID COPPERFIELD (Twentieth Century–Fox, 1970)
Produced by Frederick H. Bogger; directed by Delbert Mann; screenplay by Jack Pulman from the novel by Charles Dickens (118 minutes).
Cast: Dame Edith Evans (Aunt Betsy), Sir Michael Redgrave (Mr. Peggotty), Sir Ralph Richardson (Micawber), Wendy Hiller (Mrs. Micawber), Robin Phillips (David Copperfield), Laurence Olivier (Mr. Creakle)

NICHOLAS AND ALEXANDRA (Columbia, 1971)
Produced by Sam Spiegel and Franklin J. Schaffner; directed by Schaffner, from a screenplay by James Goldman, based on a book by Robert K. Massie (180 minutes)
Cast: Michael Jayston (Czar Nicholas of Russia), Janet Suzman (Czarina Alexandra), Harry Andrews (Grand Duke), Tom Baker (Rasputin), Michael Redgrave (Foreign Minister Sazonor), Laurence Olivier (Prime Minister Witte).
16mm. rental: Swank Motion Pictures, St. Louis, Mo.

SLEUTH (Twentieth Century–Fox, 1972)
Produced by Morton Gottlieb; directed by Joseph L. Mankiewicz; screenplay by Anthony Shaffer from his play of the same title (135 minutes)
Cast: Laurence Olivier (Andrew Wyke), Michael Caine (Milo Tindle)
16mm. rental: Films, Inc.

LADY CAROLINE LAMB (Tomorrow Entertainment, 1973)
Produced by Fernando Ghia; directed by Robert Bolt, from his own
    screenplay (123 minutes)
Cast: Sarah Miles (Lady Caroline Lamb), Jon Finch (William Lamb),
    Richard Chamberlain (Lord Byron), John Mills (Canning), Margaret
    Leighton (Lady Melbourne), Ralph Richardson (King George IV),
    Laurence Olivier (Duke of Wellington)

LOVE AMONG THE RUINS (Paramount-TV-ABC Circle Films, 1975)
Produced by Alan Davis; directed by George Cukor, from a script by James
    Costigan (120 minutes)
Cast: Katharine Hepburn (Jessica Medlicott), Sir Laurence Olivier (Sir Ar-
    thur Granville-Jones, K.C.), Colin Blakely (J. F. Devine, K.C.),
    Richard Pearson (Bruce)
(Note: premiered on ABC-TV, March 6, 1975, under the sponsorship of
    IBM.

MARATHON MAN (Paramount, 1976)
Produced by Robert Evans and Sidney Beckerman; directed by John
    Schlesinger; screenplay by William Goldman, from his novel of the
    same title (125 minutes)
Cast: Dustin Hoffman (Babe), Roy Schieder (Brother), Laurence Olivier
    (Szell), Marthe Keller (Girl Friend)
16mm. rental: RBC/Paramount

THE SEVEN PER CENT SOLUTION (Universal, 1976)
Produced and directed by Herbert Ross, from a screenplay by Nicholas
    Meyer, based on his novel; music by John Addison, with "The
    Madame's Song" by Stephen Sondheim (113 minutes)
Cast: Nicol Williamson (Sherlock Holmes), Robert Duvall (Dr. Watson),
    Alan Arkin (Sigmund Freud), Laurence Olivier (Professor Moriarty).
    Vanessa Redgrave (Lois Devereaux), Joel Grey (Lowenstein)
16mm. rental: Universal 16

A BRIDGE TOO FAR (United Artists, 1977)
Produced by Joseph E. Levine and Richard P. Levine; directed by Richard
    Attenborough; screenplay by William Goldman, from a book by Cor-
    nelius Ryan.
Cast: Dirk Bogarde (Browning), James Caan (Dohur), Sean Connery (Maj.
    Gen Urquhart), Laurence Olivier (Dr. Spaander), Elliot Gould (Col.
    Short), Ryan O'Neal (Brig. Gen. Gavin), Robert Redford (Maj. Julian
    Cook), Liv Ullmann (Kate ter Horst)
16mm. rental: United Artists 16

THE BETSY (Allied Artists, 1978)
Produced by Robert Weston; directed by Daniel Petrie; screenplay by
  William Blast and Walter Bernsetin, based on a novel of the same title
  by Harold Robbins (125 minutes)
Cast: Laurence Olivier (Loren Hardeman, Sr.), Lesley-Anne Down (Lady
  Bobby Ayres), Katharine Ross (Sally Hardeman), Robert Duvall (Loren
  Hardeman, III)

THE BOYS FROM BRAZIL (Twentieth Century–Fox, 1978)
Produced by Martin Richards and Stanley O'Toole; directed by Franklin J.
  Schaffner; screenplay by Kenneth Ross and Heywood Gould, based on
  a book by Ira Levin
Cast: James Mason, Laurence Olivier, Gregory Peck, Lilli Palmer

A LITTLE ROMANCE (Warner Brothers, 1979)
Produced by Yves Rousset-Rouard and Robert L. Crawford; directed by
  George Roy Hills; screenplay by Allan Burns, based on the novel
  $E = Mc^2$, *Mon Amour* by Patrick Cauvin.
Cast: Laurence Olivier, Thelonious Bernard, Diane Lane, Arthur Hill,
  Sally Kellerman, Arlene Franics, Broderick Crawford.

DRACULA (Universal, 1979)
Produced by Walter Mirisch and John Badham; directed by John
  Badham; screenplay by W. D. Richter, based on the stage play by
  Hamilton Deane and John L. Balderston from the novel by Bram
  Stoker.
Cast: Frank Langella, Laurence Olivier, Donald Pleasence, Kate
  Nelligan, Jan Francis.

INCHON (One Way, 1980)
Produced by Rev. Moon and Mitsuharu Ishi; directed by Terence Young;
  screenplay by Robin Moore, Laird Koenig, Barry Beckerman.
Cast: Laurence Olivier, Jacqueline Bisset, Ben Gazzara, Omar Sharif,
  Toshiro Mifune.

THE JAZZ SINGER (EMI, 1980)
Produced by Jerry Leider; directed by Richard Fleischer; screenplay by
  Stephen Forman, Herbert Baker.
Cast: Neil Diamond, Laurence Olivier, Lucy Arnez.

CLASH OF THE TITANS (Metro-Goldwyn-Mayer, 1981)
Produced by Charles H. Schneer and Ray Harryhausen; directed by
  Desmond David; screenplay by Beverly Cross.
Cast: Ursula Andress, Burgess Meredith, Harry Hamlin, Flora Robson,
  Claire Bloom, Laurence Olivier, Maggie Smith, Tim Piggot-Smith.

Index

187

Other Da Capo titles of interest